The Quiet Home

House Hushing for Calm and Intentional Living

Aesop.
LIVE BEAUTIFUL
SOFT MINIMAL
ARRANGING THINGS
ROSE UNIACKE AT WORK

The Quiet Home

House Hushing for Calm and Intentional Living

MITCHELL
BEAZLEY

Michelle Halford

First published in Great Britain in 2026
by Mitchell Beazley,
an imprint of Octopus Publishing Group Ltd
Carmelite House
50 Victoria Embankment
London EC4Y 0DZ
www.octopusbooks.co.uk

An Hachette UK Company
www.hachette.co.uk

The authorized representative in the EEA
is Hachette Ireland, 8 Castlecourt Centre,
Dublin 15, D15 XTP3, Ireland (email: info@hbgi.ie)

Copyright © 2026 Quarto Publishing plc.
Text Copyright © 2026 Michelle Halford

Distributed in the US by Hachette Book Group
1290 Avenue of the Americas, 4th and 5th Floors
New York, NY 10104, USA

Distributed in Canada by Canadian Manda Group
664 Annette St., Toronto, Ontario, Canada M6S 2C8

Michelle Halford has asserted her moral right to be identified as the Author of this Work in accordance with the Copyright Designs and Patents Act 1988.

All rights reserved. No part of this book may be reproduced or utilized in any form or by any means, electronic or mechanical, including photocopying, recording or by any information storage and retrieval system, without the prior written permission of the publisher.

Every effort has been made to trace the copyright holders of material quoted in this book. If application is made in writing to the publisher, any omissions will be included in future editions.

ISBN 978-1-78472-982-0
eISBN 978-1-78472-983-7

A CIP catalogue record for this book
is available from the British Library.

Conceived, edited and designed by
Quintessence Editions,
an imprint of The Quarto Group
1 Triptych Place
London SE1 9SH
www.quarto.com

QUAR.1179690

Senior commissioning editor: Jo Lightfoot
Senior editor: Kath Stathers
Copyeditor: Jodi Simpson
Design: Sarah Pyke
Picture research: Claire Holland
Production manager: David Hearn
Managing editor: Emma Harverson
Art director: Gemma Wilson
Publisher, Quintessence: Eszter Karpati
Publisher: Lorraine Dickey

Printed and bound in China

10 9 8 7 6 5 4 3 2 1

Contents

How do you hush a home?

Have you ever wondered why some homes radiate calm and tranquillity, appearing to whisper rather than shout? The answer lies in the concept of the quiet home, which extends beyond aesthetics to encompass a deeper understanding of the elements that shape interior spaces and the profound impact they have on our physical and emotional well-being.

In an era when life is fast-paced and driven by technology, our homes offer a welcome respite from overstimulation and the bustling outside world. Yet, as life gets busier, our homes often suffer too, with growing visual noise in the form of clutter, general excess and a myriad of distractions. This accumulation often happens gradually: one day a room that once felt calm begins to feel stifling, its surfaces crowded, its corners filled with objects that serve no purpose. Over time, this disruption in our spaces can take a toll on our mental health. Taking cues from house hushing techniques that have gained momentum in recent times, this book provides strategies for reducing visual chaos, fostering beautiful, calming interiors and cultivating a slower, more grounded life.

But house hushing isn't simply about decluttering – it's about making space for what truly matters, allowing the essential elements of a home to breathe. If you've ever walked into a room and felt a sense of unease, chances are the interior was filled with competing voices – too many objects vying for attention, an imbalance of colour or a layout that disrupted the natural flow of movement. In contrast, a thoughtfully arranged space invites stillness; it allows the eye to rest, the mind to quiet and the body to settle.

Research has shown that our physical surroundings directly influence our emotional state. Clutter, for example, has been linked to heightened stress levels and decreased focus, while harmonious, well-balanced environments can enhance relaxation and productivity. A hushed home isn't just visually serene – it actively

supports well-being by reducing unnecessary stimulation and creating spaces where the mind can recalibrate.

Beyond what we see, a hushed home is also about what we feel, hear and even smell. Soft, natural textiles underfoot, the absence of harsh acoustics and the delicate scent of fresh air or natural materials all contribute to a space that feels restorative. The gentle texture of linen, the warmth of wood or the coolness of smooth stone - these elements are more than just aesthetic choices; they shape our daily experience in quiet, profound ways.

In a world where we are constantly absorbing information, often without realizing it, an environment that soothes rather than stimulates becomes an essential counterbalance. A quiet home is not about emptiness or a lack of creativity; it is about cultivating an atmosphere where every element is considered, intentional and supportive of a deeper sense of calm.

If you imagine that everything in a room has a voice, and that voice is taking up visual, physical and mental space, the act of dialling down the noise - through thoughtful considerations of interior elements such as colour, materials, forms and light - can promote increased presence, focus and happiness.

This process doesn't mean stripping a space of personality or removing all decorative elements. Rather, it's about understanding how each piece contributes to the overall feeling of a room. Does a certain object bring a sense of joy, reflecting you and what you love, or does it add to a feeling of visual clutter? Does the colour palette encourage restfulness, or does it introduce a level of energy that feels out of sync with the room's intended mood? Thoughtful choices - prioritizing quality over excess, embracing a balance of old and new - help shape a home that feels both inviting and distinctly yours.

The idea of creating a quiet home is not new. Many cultures have long valued interiors that foster peace and simplicity. The Japanese philosophy of *wabi-sabi*, for instance, embraces imperfection and the beauty of the understated. Scandinavian *hygge* centres on warmth, comfort and an unhurried way of living. Even ancient monastic spaces, with their emphasis on restraint and balance, offer inspiration for how our surroundings can support a contemplative, intentional life.

While design trends may shift, the desire for a home that nurtures rather than overwhelms remains constant. A hushed home is not about adhering to a particular style, but rather about fostering an atmosphere that resonates with your own sense of balance and comfort – tuning in to what feels right, quieting what feels excessive and creating a home that serves as a true retreat.

Two of the most powerful tools in house hushing are light and space. Natural light is crucial; as it shifts throughout the day, it creates a dynamic interplay of softness and shadow that gently enhances the mood of a space. Working with light – whether through sheer curtains, reflective surfaces or the strategic placement of furniture – promotes this natural rhythm, bringing spaces to life and creating a sense of openness. Every area of the home should encourage flow and allow the eye to move freely, with thoughtfully layered textures adding depth and warmth without overwhelming. Negative space is just as important as the objects within an interior; knowing when to leave a surface bare or allow a corner to remain unfilled creates balance and breathing room.

For some, the process of house hushing might mean an entire home reset, methodically reassessing each room to create a greater sense of calm and well-being. For others, it might be a more gradual refinement – paring back a shelf, introducing more natural materials or rethinking how a space is used. Even small shifts can have a noticeable impact: clearing a cluttered surface or simplifying a colour palette can subtly transform a space. There is no rigid formula, only an ongoing practice of paying attention to what enhances daily life and letting go of what doesn't.

In the pages that follow, core interior elements are unpacked and interwoven through a variety of methods, providing you with a diverse toolkit to create an intentional home sanctuary that fosters tranquillity and calm amid the chaos of modern life. Whether you're styling a sideboard, refreshing a room or undertaking a full-scale build or renovation, you'll uncover nuanced and thoughtful strategies – from achieving a harmonious balance of colours and the soothing embrace of natural materials, through to harnessing the power of natural light and the gentle whispers of space – to nurture your well-being and enrich everyday life.

Chapter one

Foundations

At the heart of the quiet home are five key principles that guide the creation of calm, intentional spaces. Whether you're approaching a full renovation or simply refreshing a single room, these foundations offer a practical framework that can be applied at any scale to create homes that feel both serene and deeply personal.

In today's accelerated world, our homes are more than just places to live – they are sanctuaries, workspaces and havens for connection. Yet, when filled with too much noise – visual, physical or emotional – our spaces can begin to feel overwhelming. The principles of house hushing address that noise, helping you strip away the unnecessary and focus on what brings clarity and comfort.

Soothing colour palettes lay the groundwork for a quiet home by calming the senses and creating a cohesive flow from room to room. Natural materials like wood, stone and linen connect us to the outdoors, fostering a sense of grounding and ease. Tactility invites us to engage with our spaces through touch, layering textures that add depth and intrigue. Soft curves and organic forms offset the clean lines of modern interiors, echoing the gentle rhythms found in nature. Lastly, flexibility ensures that our spaces can adapt to our changing needs, offering both function and freedom through thoughtful, versatile interiors.

Paving the way for a deeper exploration in the chapters that follow, these foundations are not a set of rules, but rather guiding ideas that form the basis of a quieter home – one that nurtures well-being, invites calm and allows you to fully exhale the moment you walk through the door.

Soothing palettes

Colour profoundly shapes how we feel, think and behave, making it one of the most powerful tools in decorating. Its influence reaches beyond aesthetics, affecting mood, atmosphere and even how we interact with our surroundings. In the quiet home, the careful selection of colours becomes an essential foundation for creating spaces that evoke calm and foster well-being. Soft, neutral hues create a sense of ease, offering a backdrop that feels understated yet warm. When carried throughout the home, a cohesive palette enhances fluidity and brings a quiet harmony, creating spaces that feel intentionally composed.

Colour is more than decoration – it resonates with us on an emotional and psychological level. It reflects personal style while shaping the atmosphere of a room. Thoughtful colour choices can support both the function of a space and the moods of those who live there.

Neutral tones as a framework

Neutral tones have a unique ability to create balance and harmony. Inherent in nature, these muted shades – dusty, powdery and understated – mirror the subtle shifts in light we experience daily. This softness prevents overstimulation, allowing the senses to settle. And while neutral shades are subdued, they needn't feel flat or monotonous; undertones – the subtle hues that lie beneath a colour's surface – add depth, creating gentle variations that draw the eye in, revealing delicate nuances.

It is these undertones that quietly influence how a shade appears under different lighting and when paired with other colours. Neutrals – whether warm or cool – are timeless, versatile and profoundly calming. Warm neutrals such as creams, beiges and earthy browns evoke a sense of comfort and ease, while cooler tones such as soft greys and muted blues feel sophisticated and soothing. Matched together, these hues can create sanctuaries of peace, and are ideal for making spaces dedicated to rest and rejuvenation.

Striking the right balance is essential for a cohesive space. This means deciding on either a predominantly warm or cool palette, then introducing subtle accents from the opposite spectrum to add contrast and depth. For example, a space grounded in purely cool tones may feel detached or cold. The addition of warm accents - through textiles or natural materials - helps create a more balanced and engaging space.

Neutral tones provide a versatile foundation - minimal yet multifaceted, they allow materials and textures to stand out. Incorporating timber, stone and soft textiles adds dimension to the neutral palette, ensuring it feels layered and dynamic. Regardless of style - whether contemporary or traditional, Nordic minimalist or mid-century modern - neutral tones offer a timeless base that allows for continuous evolution.

How they are applied makes all the difference. Rich neutrals can add depth and complexity to a space, while lighter shades can refresh a tired interior, creating an airy and welcoming atmosphere. Subtle tonal shifts can highlight traditional architectural details like architraves and fireplaces, while a single, seamless neutral creates a soft, understated backdrop for furniture and finishes in a refined, contemporary setting.

Another advantage of a neutral palette is its adaptability. As your home evolves, neutrals provide the flexibility to introduce new accent colours, textures or patterns. Small seasonal changes - such as fresh flowers - become effortless, while larger updates, like new curtains, can be easily added but remain harmonious within the established palette.

Spatial perception

Colour doesn't just influence emotions - it shapes our perception of space. Lighter hues reflect light, making rooms feel more expansive, while darker tones absorb light, creating a sense of intimacy. Warm colours visually draw walls closer, making a space feel enveloping, while cooler tones recede, creating the illusion of openness. Painting the ceiling the same colour as the walls can blur boundaries, drawing the eye upwards, subtly elongating the space.

Within a neutral palette, these principles can guide colour placement in different areas of your home. Warmer neutrals in living areas encourage both social interaction and cosiness, while cooler tones in the bedroom can promote relaxation and rest. In the kitchen, warmer hues can inspire both culinary creativity and connection.

Building a unified palette of neutrals

Neutral palettes transcend trends, bringing enduring appeal that can evolve with your home. From the ancient use of ochre pigments to today's eco-friendly paints, the quiet beauty of neutrals remains a timeless thread in considered homes.

To create a cohesive home, start with a limited palette of three to four neutrals. A strong foundation typically begins with one dominant neutral, such as beige, paired with a secondary hue, such as off-white, for smaller design elements. Then, introduce one or two accent shades - darker tones, like brown or black, that add contrast and visual depth. This provides structure while allowing for thoughtful layering of lighter and deeper variations within the same palette.

Mood boards are an invaluable tool when refining your palette. A digital collection of reference images is a useful starting point, but a physical board with paint and material swatches will give a more accurate sense of how colours translate in real life. Defining a palette early on provides a roadmap for weaving colour throughout your home, ensuring all spaces feel connected.

Through the process of house hushing, you can assess your space holistically - considering the movement of natural light, any structural elements and existing finishes such as flooring and cabinetry. Your colour palette becomes a guide, helping you to determine what stays, what no longer resonates and what new elements will bring balance.

Depth can be introduced through tonal layering - darker and richer variations of your chosen neutrals introduced through furniture, textiles and finishing touches. If you are drawn to deeper hues, consider tying them into the broader palette with subtle accents. For instance, a muted burgundy paint colour in the bedroom can be echoed with flowers in the living room or ceramics in the kitchen.

Extend this cohesion by blurring the lines between interior and exterior spaces. Continuity in materials - such as carrying stone flooring through from inside to out - or using upholstery in complementary tones, creates a seamless transition.

An effective neutral palette supports the evolving home, allowing you to move decorative accents from one room to another with ease. Taking the time to refine your palette selection ensures longevity, and a home that won't feel dated in a few years. Once your palette is in place, the next step is choosing the ideal paint colour to bring it to life.

Choosing the right neutral paint shade

Look at room orientation and light

Understanding how natural light moves through your space is key to choosing the right neutral paint. Some rooms will be naturally brighter than others, and light shifts continuously throughout the day, affecting how colours appear. In sun-filled spaces, a wide range of neutrals can work – from fresh, airy hues with cool blue undertones to warmer shades that deepen in full sunlight. However, bright light can amplify warm undertones like yellow and red, so if you're aiming for balance, cooler neutrals may be a better fit.

In contrast, naturally dark rooms with minimal light can feel flat with cool-toned neutrals. To prevent this, avoid shades with green, grey or blue bases, since they can make the space feel cold. Instead, opt for warmer neutrals with red, yellow or pink undertones to soften shadows and create a cosier feel. The goal is to temper bright rooms and add warmth where light is lacking, ensuring a harmonious backdrop for your decor.

For rooms where natural light shifts dramatically – bright in the morning, darker in the afternoon – choose a neutral that works well in both settings. Think about when you use the space most and select a shade that enhances its atmosphere during those hours. For example, if a room is primarily used in the morning, choose a shade that works with bright light. If evenings are when you spend the most time there, select a tone that complements softer, dimmer light. A well-chosen neutral will subtly shift in hue throughout the day, adapting to its surroundings.

Consider existing materials

Look at how the neutral colour interacts with key elements in the room – woodwork, textiles, flooring, furniture and architectural details. Will it provide a harmonious backdrop for your artwork? Neutrals are chameleonic, shifting in appearance based on their surroundings. For instance, a stone-hued neutral with warm brown undertones can beautifully complement an interior rich in organic textures – wood flooring, earthy tiles and marble surfaces, and furnishings in beige, caramel and deep brown tones. Paying attention to these relationships ensures your chosen shade enhances, rather than clashes with, the existing design.

Test your paint

Before committing to a shade, it's essential to test it in the space. View it in large swatches – small paint chips won't give an accurate impression. Either paint directly onto the wall or use large white cards with removable tape, allowing you to move them around. I like this method because it lets you see how the colour behaves in different areas, from the brightest spots near windows to the darker corners, while also comparing different shades side by side. Observe the colour from all angles, at varying distances and at different times of day. If the room is used at night, check how it looks under artificial lighting. Your chosen colour should work well under the light in which it will most frequently be seen.

Create smooth transitions

A seamless flow from room to room enhances the sense of calm and cohesion in a home. This doesn't mean that every space needs to be the same colour, but using consistent undertones helps unify spaces. For example, if one room is painted beige with a slight green undertone, an adjacent room painted in an off-white with a similar undertone will maintain a smooth transition. In open-plan spaces, architectural features like archways can guide where one shade ends and another begins.

Subtly contrasting colours can also define key architectural elements - mouldings, wall panelling or fireplace surrounds - without disrupting the flow. Alternatively, a single, unified colour can enhance openness, with contrast introduced through décor and furnishings. For added cohesion, repeat the same approach throughout your home, even when varying colours. A consistent base colour in hallways and transition spaces further strengthens the sense of continuity.

Select the ideal finish

While there are no strict rules, factors like durability and sheen should guide your choice of finish. Matte paints are popular for high-traffic areas like living rooms and hallways, since they are durable and non-reflective, helping to conceal imperfections. Gloss finishes, however, create a striking contrast when paired with matte walls, adding depth to architectural elements or bringing light into a darker space.

Chalky or lime-wash finishes also work beautifully with neutral palettes, lending a subtle depth to walls. In areas exposed to moisture, speciality paints for wet environments are essential. Opt for paints low in volatile organic compounds (VOCs) for a healthier indoor environment.

Natural elements

Time spent in nature offers a profound sense of calm and renewal, easing stress and restoring balance. Studies show that natural environments have tangible benefits for both mind and body, lowering cortisol levels and improving overall well-being. Translating this connection into our homes is essential to creating spaces that feel quiet, restorative and deeply nurturing. Through the thoughtful use of natural materials, the introduction of greenery or fresh flowers and the intentional design of light-filled interiors, we can cultivate homes that embody these principles.

Natural elements form the foundation of a calming home, from the grounding presence of wood and stone to the transformative power of light. By weaving these elements into both the structure and the softer layers of a space, you can create interiors that feel alive, balanced and connected to the world beyond their walls.

A return to nature

For most of human history, daily life was shaped by the rhythms of the natural world – the rising and setting of the sun, the changing seasons and the landscapes we inhabited. Today, however, many of us move through life in a way that requires little connection to nature. While convenient, this separation can leave us feeling unmoored, affecting both our well-being and sense of place.

Though no indoor space can fully replicate the experience of being in nature, research shows that bringing elements of the natural world indoors can significantly enhance our comfort and reduce stress. Whether it's the warmth of sunlight streaming through a window, the grainy texture of a timber floor or the quiet beauty of a plant-filled corner, these connections ground us, offering moments of calm amid the busyness of life.

A home designed to support both physical and mental well-being begins with natural materials and a connection to light. Consider sustainability alongside comfort, and incorporate elements such as organic fabrics, responsibly sourced wood and natural stone, fostering a tactile connection to the earth and creating spaces that feel intentional and harmonious. The grain of wood tells a story, responding beautifully to light and lending character to floors, furniture and cabinetry. Whether smooth or textured, natural stone has an enduring quality, anchoring a space with its strength and presence.

Maximizing daylight enhances mood and brings a dynamic quality to interiors, shifting with the time of day and season. Fresh air is just as essential, helping to create a home that feels as healthy as it is inviting. Thoughtful ventilation, non-toxic materials and low-VOC finishes all contribute to better air quality. By weaving these elements together, a home becomes an extension of the natural world - a space that supports healing and restoration.

Light is essential in creating spaces that feel alive, bringing out the depth and warmth of materials like wood and stone. Rooms filled with light evolve throughout the day, responding to changes in weather and season. By framing views and allowing light to flood in, a home feels open and connected to its surroundings. Thoughtful use of light, paired with a restrained material palette, generates a sense of calm and respite.

Greenery and flowers

Plants and flowers bring life and movement to interiors and are known to improve our mood. Greenery adds texture and colour, and flowers offer a sensory experience through their beauty and fragrance. Whether freshly picked from the garden or sourced locally, they provide an effortless way to introduce nature into the home. There's no need for an elaborate arrangement - sometimes a few stems from the garden or foraged branches can create the most striking, organic feel.

Materials that ground

Natural materials bring a quiet honesty to the home. A refined palette of timber, stone and organic textiles celebrates texture and imperfection, adding depth and richness to interiors. Wood, in particular, has long been a cornerstone of interior design, valued for its warmth, durability and versatility. A living material, it evolves with time, and its natural grain and knots provide distinctive character and inherent beauty. From architectural elements like flooring and beams to furniture and smaller decorative accents, wood fosters a connection to nature in a way that feels both timeless and grounding.

Beyond its beauty, wood offers environmental benefits as well. When sourced responsibly, it is a renewable material with a lower environmental impact than alternatives such as concrete or steel. It also has natural insulating properties, helping to regulate temperature and reduce energy use. Studies suggest that wooden environments can even lower blood pressure and pulse rates, underscoring their potential to enhance well-being.

With the right balance, wood elements can unify a space or create moments of contrast - whether you're introducing a single statement piece or layering a mix of tones and finishes. Its versatility means it can be tailored to suit different rooms and needs, offering subtle warmth in a bedroom, sculptural interest in a hallway or visual rhythm in a kitchen or dining area. However it's used, wood has a grounding effect, bringing tactile depth and quiet integrity to the spaces in which we live.

Using wood in the home

Flooring

Wooden flooring is a timeless choice, infusing spaces with warmth and character. Traditional hardwoods offer a wide variety of options, from unique colours, grains and textures to styles such as plank, herringbone or chevron, allowing for a personalized look and feel. Durable and easy to maintain, wood flooring also ages beautifully. For a sustainable approach, consider cork or reclaimed wood, or revive older hardwood floors by sanding and refinishing them with a stain or sealant.

Wall cladding

Timber-clad walls or panelling can act like a warm embrace, introducing texture through a variety of styles to suit both contemporary and traditional aesthetics. Slim slatted timber panels complement minimal spaces, while wainscoting adds charm to classic interiors. Veneer panels offer a sustainable, cost-effective alternative to solid wood, with brushed, sawn or smooth finishes.

Panelling can cover entire walls or be used as half-wall accents to inject contrast or create shelving. Directional choices can visually alter a space: vertical planks add height, while horizontal boards create a sense of spaciousness. Ceiling panels in natural wood can also bring texture and warmth, with minimal maintenance required over time.

Furniture

Quality wood furniture is synonymous with craftsmanship and enduring elegance. Whether you prefer sleek contemporary lines or bold rounded forms, the richness of walnut or the light tones of oak, each piece carries its own unique grain patterns and textures, making it inherently one of a kind. From larger pieces like dining tables, bookshelves and bed frames, to smaller accents such as stools and side tables, wood furniture blends beauty and functionality, adding depth and calm to a space. Sustainability is another hallmark of wood furniture. Look for pieces that are crafted from responsibly sourced wood, and mix vintage with modern for an authentic, layered feel.

Decorative elements

Consider using wood for small-scale elements and finishing touches. A simple floating shelf ties design elements together while providing a practical display solution. Handcrafted wooden pieces, such as bowls, candleholders and sculptures, bring organic beauty and reflect artisanal craftsmanship. Even a wooden frame for artwork can enhance a space with its natural texture.

Exposed beams
Whether rustic or refined, exposed wooden beams inject character and contrast against a neutral backdrop. They can also enhance the feeling of height and space. Reclaimed wood beams, sourced from old buildings or industrial spaces, offer sustainability and charm. Reclaimed wood can also be repurposed for doors, shelves and furniture, blending heritage with contemporary style.

Mixing different wood tones
As you accumulate pieces over time, don't shy away from combining light and dark woods. A curated mix of wood tones adds to a layered, personal feel. To maintain cohesion, focus on subtle similarities in undertones, finishes or grain patterns.

Bespoke solutions
Celebrate the versatility of timber with custom woodwork such as built-in shelving, cabinetry or a kitchen island. Pair these with contrasting materials like stone or metal to create a harmonious blend of textures, adding depth and elegance to your space.

Tactility

A truly calming home extends beyond the visual to engage all the senses - particularly touch, which is fundamental to how we experience a space. Tactility, or the haptic experience, refers to the relationship between touch and material properties - how textures, temperatures and surfaces shape our connection to our environment and our homes. In a world dominated by digital interactions, reconnecting with our sense of touch through our surroundings has never been more important to our well-being. By embracing texture and materiality, we create spaces that resonate on a deeper level, offering a retreat from the overstimulation of modern life.

As Finnish architect Juhani Pallasmaa writes in *The Eyes of the Skin*, 'Every touching experience of architecture is multi-sensory.' Touch is our first sense to develop - even before birth - and plays a crucial role in childhood, helping us to understand the world around us. Our skin's receptors respond not only to texture and temperature but also on an emotional level. Interpersonal touch releases oxytocin, a hormone linked to love and social bonding, reinforcing the deep connection between physical contact, comfort and a sense of belonging.

Studies show that our sensitivity to tactile stimuli is not only psychological but deeply ingrained in our physiology. When a space lacks tactile richness, we simply inhabit it rather than truly experiencing it. Thoughtful use of texture allows us to feel immersed in our spaces, making them warm, inviting and deeply personal.

Materials shaped by human hands or nature's slow processes carry a certain resonance - they remind us of what is real. Linen softened over time, hand-thrown ceramics with subtle imperfections or the worn grain of timber all invite touch and connection. These textures tell stories of place and craft, helping us to build emotional attachment to our spaces, anchoring us in the present while gently evoking past experiences. In this way, tactile design becomes a form of storytelling - one that unfolds not through words but through the surfaces we live alongside every day. It encourages us to slow down, to notice, to feel.

CHANEL
VOGUE

Sensory connection

Our senses interact with spaces in layered, complex ways. Like scent or sound, touch can evoke memories and emotions - transporting us to a cherished destination, recalling significant moments or symbolizing love and connection. A home's textures take on meaning through personal experience, shaping the way we perceive and connect with our surroundings.

Practice restraint in the number of items you select when curating a space, but be generous in the tactile quality of the pieces you choose. Ask what can be removed, but just as importantly, ask what is essential. The right materials bring a home to life, ensuring it feels as good as it looks while reflecting your own vision of calm.

Texture and materiality

Tactility begins with materials that ground us in nature, their touch bringing warmth and depth to a space. The feeling of a natural jute rug underfoot, the smooth grain of a wooden benchtop or the cool surface of veined marble connects us to the physicality of our environment. These materials stand the test of time, aging beautifully and developing a patina that tells a story - a brass doorknob bearing the traces to those who have passed through, an oak dining table marked by years of shared meals, a wool throw that has provided warmth season after season. Tactility reminds us that homes are meant to be lived in.

Contrasts, especially in texture, bring intrigue and interest to interiors. Mix smooth with rough, such as a velvet sofa paired with a textured wool cushion, or shiny with matte, like a polished stainless steel teapot beside stoneware cups. A woven basket on a smooth wooden shelf or textured placemats next to sleek ceramic tableware create a dynamic interplay that captures the eye and invites touch.

Even understated interiors can be rich in materiality. Rendered plaster walls provide a smooth, tactile backdrop, while a thoughtfully pared-back curation of pieces celebrates natural materials like wood, linen, clay and stone. Stone, in particular, balances elegance with raw, earthy beauty - its variations and imperfections add to its richness. Whether used for flooring, tiles, benchtops or sculptural elements like bookends and bowls, different types of stone - marble, travertine, granite, limestone - offer a range of textures, from smooth and polished to rough-hewn. Stone's cool, grounded presence is softened when paired with the warmth of natural wood, creating a harmonious balance of textures that enhances the sensory experience of a space.

When combining stone and wood, consider how tone, texture and finish can work together to create both contrast and cohesion. A richly veined stone benchtop might be balanced by smooth, minimally grained timber cabinetry, allowing each material to stand out without competing. Warm-toned travertine pairs beautifully with darker woods, adding depth and richness, while pale marble alongside light oak or ash lends itself to a softer, more serene effect. These considered pairings highlight the natural beauty of each element while ensuring a harmonious and layered space.

Fabric selections play a key role in a home's tactility, layering warmth, softening hard surfaces and fostering a sense of calm. Natural fibres like linen, wool and organic cotton introduce varied textures and a timeless quality. Used in upholstery, window treatments, bedding, table linens and throws, these materials enrich a space with both beauty and comfort. Beyond aesthetics, natural textiles are versatile, hypoallergenic and long-lasting. When choosing fabrics, certifications like the Global Organic Textile Standard (GOTS) and OEKO-TEX Standard 100 can help you to ensure ethical sourcing and minimal chemical use, supporting both well-being and sustainability.

By quieting our homes and reducing visual noise, we amplify the presence of texture, materiality and the sensory comfort of touch. Thoughtfully chosen tactile elements transform a space into a sanctuary in which every surface invites connection, every material tells a story and every detail contributes to a sense of calm and belonging.

Soft shapes

A hushed interior is shaped not just by what we include, but how we include it. While clean lines and structured forms bring clarity, they can also create a feeling of rigidity. Softening these edges with curves and rounded forms results in spaces that feel more fluid, inviting and serene. Drawing on biophilic design, which connects our homes to the natural world, we can create interiors that breathe - spaces that feel alive and restorative.

At its core, biophilic design taps into our innate connection to nature. One of its key principles is the use of shapes and forms that mimic the complexity found outdoors - organic curves, circular patterns and flowing silhouettes. Our affinity for these forms spans centuries, seen in everything from ancient architecture to modernist design. Architects and designers have long looked to nature for inspiration, finding beauty in the intricate patterns of flowers, the smooth contours of stones, the gentle rise of hills and the undulating lines of rivers.

Research has shown that we gravitate towards soft shapes because they signal safety and comfort. In contrast, too many rectilinear forms and sharp angles can feel harsh and overstimulating. Curved forms soothe us, not only visually but emotionally, offering a sense of ease and relaxation. The renowned modernist sculptor Jean Arp explored this through his biomorphic works - smoothly rounded sculptures in plaster, stone and bronze that evoke nature's elegance. His pieces produce a calming, almost meditative response, much like how our hands instinctively envelop a rounded cup or trace the gentle arc of a chair.

Incorporating soft shapes into the home doesn't require grand architectural gestures, though those can certainly enhance a space. Even subtle, thoughtful additions can transform the atmosphere, bringing balance and softness to structured environments.

Introducing curves and flow

Soft shapes can be introduced in layers, from architectural elements to the smallest details. Vaulted ceilings, curved walls, arched doorways and rounded pillars bring softness to the hard geometry of a home, shifting the eye from rigid lines to flowing forms. These elements create a gentle rhythm throughout a space, encouraging a sense of movement and ease.

Smaller features can add organic touches without overwhelming a room: arched recessed wall niches to display decorative objects, a softly curved fireplace to offset a square surround or a curved kitchen island that fosters togetherness. Fixtures and fittings offer another opportunity for softness - rounded taps, a circular ceramic basin, curvy door handles or sculptural wall hooks can offset angular doors and cabinetry. Use soft shapes to complement and counteract the sharper elements in a room.

Furniture and lighting

Curved furniture softens a space and creates a natural sense of flow. Pairing it with clean lines and angular pieces enhances harmony and balance: for example, a sofa that curves subtly around the linear edge of a rectangular coffee table or round barstools that soften the clean lines of a kitchen island.

Seek out pieces that echo nature and add visual interest - like a coffee table with a playful, irregular form and softly bevelled edges, dining chairs that marry structured frames with rounded, upholstered seats or a lounge chair with gently sloping armrests. A sinuous bedhead in soft, padded fabric or an upholstered bench at the end of the bed can help transform a bedroom into a retreat. These elements soften the aesthetic while inviting touch, reinforcing the connection between shape and tactility.

Lighting is an opportunity to explore contrasts. Pair soft curves with sharp angles for a striking, sculptural effect. Add a smooth, organic shade to a wall lamp with an angular arm, or soften a minimalist pendant with a curved opal glass orb. Natural materials such as wood or ceramics add a grounded feel, while textural metal finishes introduce a modern edge.

Iconic designs like Isamu Noguchi's handcrafted paper and bamboo lamps reveal how light interacts with soft shapes, casting gentle shadows and creating atmospheric warmth. Whether through sculptural floor lamps, rounded sconces or organic pendants, lighting enhances the flow and softness of a space.

Art and objects

Decorative objects offer an easy, versatile way to introduce soft shapes. Sculptural bowls, vases and candleholders crafted from natural materials like wood, stone or metal bring both function and form to a space. Look for hand-turned wooden vessels, sphere-shaped stone accents or smooth brass bowls that reflect light and add depth. Experiment with form – mixing playful silhouettes with poetic curves and fluid waves. A scallop-edged plate, sculptural silverware, a rippled ceramic dish and wavy iron candleholders all bring a sense of movement.

Artworks can further enhance this sense of fluidity – whether through abstract paintings that explore organic forms or landscapes that echo the gentle curves found in nature. Mirrors, too, can soften a space. Arched or organically shaped, they add curves and also reflect light, making rooms feel more open and airy. Whether newly sourced or collected over time, these elements layer in texture and personality.

Remember that contrasts are key. Add a round cushion to a boxy sofa, place a sculptural object atop a square-edged plinth or mix curved ceramics with stacked books on shelves or a coffee table. These combinations create a dynamic yet cohesive feel.

Nature's touch

Finally, one of the simplest ways to incorporate soft shapes is through nature itself. Foliage, fresh or dried, adds a sculptural quality to interiors. The organic forms of branches, leaves and flowers echo the natural curves we're drawn to, reinforcing the sense of calm and connection that defines a quiet home.

Consider the scale and character of your space when choosing foliage. A single stem or gently arching branch can create a striking focal point in a minimal setting, while a fuller arrangement of natural flowers brings softness and abundance to larger spaces. Let the shape and movement of the foliage guide your display – it will feel more effortless and in tune with the surroundings.

Embracing soft shapes brings a sense of balance – grounded yet uplifting. These gentle forms, inspired by nature, create visual harmony and invite ease, turning the spaces we live in into true sanctuaries.

Flexibility

Creating a quiet home entails the ability to change and adapt. Our homes are not static; they are constantly evolving, just as we are. This means being open to the idea that our homes grow and shift alongside us, and approaching each project - whether subtle or significant - with these essential questions: How will this space be used? How do I want it to make me feel? This holistic perspective moves beyond aesthetics, fostering a mindset and a more considered way of living - one where spaces develop slowly, evoke authenticity and reflect personal style, rather than chasing trends or instant gratification.

'It is better to live in a state of impermanence than in one of finality,' wrote Gaston Bachelard in *The Poetics of Space*. When we invest passion, time and effort into crafting a calming sanctuary, the goal isn't to reach a finish line. A home isn't something to be completed or resolved entirely; instead, it should remain dynamic, with room to change. While there's satisfaction in completing a renovation or room update, the true beauty lies in the process - reworking elements like floor plans, paint colours and materials to create spaces that are adaptable, responsive to different moods and suited to varying times of day and seasons of life. Functional living spaces are those that balance social spaces for gatherings with friends and family with restorative corners for quiet reflection. Like a garden that flourishes through care and adaptation to its environment, a home thrives when it evolves with the rhythms of daily life.

Adaptable spaces allow us to grow with the changes life brings. Change, after all, is inevitable. Families expand, children grow up and move out - or move back in - elderly parents may come to live with us, and our work lives often shift. A new job might require frequent travel, or self-employment may have us working from home full-time. While this doesn't mean we're bound to stay in the same house forever, the idea of creating a home with longevity - especially one we've thoughtfully designed or made our own - is a key goal when guided by these foundations. By building flexible spaces that accommodate life's shifts, we can navigate transitions without major upheavals, whether that's

avoiding another renovation, having to replace all the furniture to suit new requirements or feeling compelled to move because our home no longer fits our needs.

So, what does flexibility mean in the context of the quiet home? It's about crafting a home that functions well and adapts to changing needs, serving as a sanctuary that supports wellness and balance. Contemporary living features fluid roles and shifting routines that come from a range of influences - remote work, evolving family dynamics and a growing emphasis on personal well-being. By designing spaces that transition effortlessly between uses, we create homes that not only meet practical demands but also nurture a sense of calm and continuity, regardless of how life unfolds.

This means making spaces that can be multifunctional - whether it's a home office that doubles as a guest bedroom or a living area that can be segregated for space to exercise, it begins with uncluttered surroundings, thoughtful spatial planning and the use of partitions, versatile furniture and clever storage integration.

Flexibility and well-being

The balance between open-plan and compartmentalized spaces plays a significant role in a wellness-focused home, shaping both the flow of movement and sense of connection within. Open layouts create an airy, spacious feel, inviting social interaction and fostering a harmonious atmosphere. In contrast, more defined spaces can provide privacy and minimize distractions, making them ideal for times of solitude and focused tasks. Introducing flexible, multi-use areas - like a living-room corner that doubles as a home office or workout zone - enhances functionality and supports a balanced lifestyle. Providing for this adaptability allows you to shape spaces to suit your personal needs, fostering a sense of control and comfort in daily life.

Social spaces within the home play a crucial role in enhancing well-being. Communal areas - such as living, dining and kitchen spaces - facilitate gatherings and meaningful interactions with family and friends. Flexible seating arrangements and warm, welcoming décor create an atmosphere where everyone feels comfortable, meals can be enjoyed and lasting memories are made.

Equally important is the creation of designated quiet areas for relaxation and reflection. Whether it's a dedicated space for Pilates or meditation, or a cosy reading nook with soft lighting and comfortable seating, these thoughtfully curated areas support personal well-being and serve as reminders to prioritize self-care in our increasingly busy lives.

Adaptable spaces should support, not dictate, how we live. By balancing areas for relaxation with spaces that encourage social connection, homes can cultivate a holistic environment that nurtures both individual peace and collective joy.

Flexible interiors are underpinned by a more intentional way of living, with thoughtful objects that are designed for daily use and built to last – not hidden away for special occasions. By buying well, choosing fewer things and ensuring items serve multiple purposes, you can reduce clutter and avoid the wasteful cycle of constant buying and discarding. This sustainable approach supports slower living, where the ability to adjust a space to meet changing needs leads to more time – a true luxury in today's fast-paced world.

Flexibility offers another important benefit: it prevents monotony and nurtures a sense of play. When our spaces are set up to encourage creativity and change – whether it's reconfiguring a room or simply restyling open shelves – it keeps our surroundings feeling fresh and inspiring. The beauty of the quiet home lies not just in what it represents today, but in the promise of what it might yet become.

Furniture

Flexible homes begin with a commitment to maintaining uncluttered surroundings and allowing space for change. A pared-back interior lends itself to flexibility, offering easy flow and adaptable options for reconfiguring without interference from excess furniture, objects or mess.

When it comes to furnishing a flexible home, longevity is key. Choose quality, well-made pieces that can evolve with your needs, offering an ever-changing narrative to your life. Consider how each piece might be used elsewhere in the home if the room is updated. While larger objects like sofas require careful planning to suit a particular space, modular styles offer greater adaptability. A bench seat is ideal paired with chairs around the dining table, but it can also be used in the hallway or bedroom. Smaller pieces, such as side tables and low stools, can transition easily between rooms – serving as extra seating, a bedside table or a convenient surface next to the sofa.

NEW FEAST
PICASSO PORTRAITS
NORDIC
PARIS MON AMOUR

Look for versatile pieces with built-in storage to help maintain an uncluttered environment. Stackable or foldable chairs can be tucked away and brought out when needed for larger gatherings, while modular shelving units can be rearranged or reconfigured. For example, a modular shelf sourced for the living room might later find a place in a child's room holding books and toys, and eventually move to a home office as your needs change.

In small spaces, consider customized furniture solutions, such as a pull-out desk for a study nook or built in bistro-style seating in the kitchen. These can provide both functionality and a beautiful, bespoke feel. Installing wall-mounted shelves, cabinets and hooks make the most of vertical space without encroaching on the room's footprint.

Movable partitions and room dividers

Room dividers offer more flexibility than structural walls, making it easy to partition or open up living areas as needed. Options range from built-in solutions like pocket or Crittall doors to freestanding, movable partitions. Transparent doors are ideal for defining spaces without blocking natural light. Crittall doors - with their slim steel frames and grid-like glass panels - introduce an industrial yet refined touch that complements both traditional and contemporary homes.

Freestanding partitions or room dividers can be folded, rotated or repositioned to define areas within a space. Use them to carve out a private workspace in the living room, create a dressing area in the bedroom or establish a cosy reading nook. Beyond dividing an open floor plan, they can double as headboards or conceal unsightly elements like exposed pipes or control panels. Even when not in use, they can act as a standalone feature, adding texture and character to a room.

Look for folding screens in woven materials, minimalist curved designs in natural wood or lightweight panels that bring softness and warmth. For something truly unique, hunt for vintage or antique finds. Mid-century designs in teak, cane or wicker, French art deco tambour styles, geometric ironwork and lacquered finishes can lend a distinct personality to your space. A curtain can also be used to divide spaces, beautifully softening the room while offering privacy. Tall bookshelves can double as room dividers too, providing storage for books and decorative objects while subtly defining zones.

Layout and circulation

Careful planning ensures that spaces adapt without disrupting the natural flow of movement. Prioritize clear, logical pathways that connect different areas of the home, avoiding obstacles and maintaining accessibility. Cohesive design elements can distinguish one area from another while preserving a unified look and feel throughout the space.

Begin with a foundational colour story - a calm base that supports visual continuity and guides the placement of furniture and objects. Vary the scale of furniture and objects to avoid visual clutter, and refine as you go, keeping only what supports flow and function. Trial and error is part of the process; arranging pieces in situ often reveals the most intuitive layout. Rather than adhering to specific styles or periods, think of your home as a living composition - one that evolves to support movement, connection and calm.

Ask yourself practical questions about how you use your rooms. Is a dedicated guest bedroom worth it if it's only used a few times a year? Could the space function better as a home office or a dual-purpose room? If renovating, would removing a wall to expand the bathroom make more sense for your lifestyle? Rooms should feel alive with use - spaces that sit idle can create a sense of stagnation. Understanding what matters most to you and those you live with will help you determine how best to shape your home.

Chapter two

Mindful minimalism

Quiet interiors are guided by a form of minimalism that is mindful and multifaceted. Taking a 'less is more' approach, the act of paring things down and eliminating the unnecessary will distil a space to its essential elements, but it isn't just about stripping away; it's a journey of intentionality and upkeep, a deliberate curation of spaces that reflect your values and the things you love, where every item has purpose and meaning. Being mindful and embracing a slower, simpler life encourages you to find joy in the quiet moments of every day. It means making considered choices and steering away from passing trends in favour of honest design, natural materials and enduring beauty. While a certain level of refinement is required to achieve quiet luxury, it's not just about aesthetics; it's about creating spaces that feel good to be in – understated, yet layered with considered elements that bring warmth and texture to invite comfort and relaxation, allowing space for contemplation and reflection amid the hectic pace of urban life. It's about decluttering, yes, but it's also about retaining items that hold significance and those that celebrate history – from vintage pieces and thoughtfully upcycled furniture to carefully curated pieces that speak to your soul. In this way you will create a home that not only brings a sense of calm and the ability to live more in the moment, but one that is imbued with layers of life and character. A home that is not just as a collection of minimalist spaces but a sanctuary for intentional living, honouring timeless pieces and embracing a philosophy grounded in the beauty of simplicity.

Decluttering

Clutter isn't just about the discomfort and inconvenience of living in untidy spaces; it culminates in visual chaos that can greatly impact our mental well-being. Numerous studies show that clutter can cause increased stress, with some showing direct links to heightened cortisol levels in people who perceive their homes as disorganized or too full. Beyond reducing stress, purposeful decluttering of your home offers many benefits – it can improve sleep quality, enhance productivity and even alleviate feelings of anxiety and depression.

A mindful approach

Taking a mindful approach to decluttering means carefully considering every item to ensure that it is truly necessary and that it contributes to the overall harmony of the space – one that is calm, elegant and meaningful. Architect John Pawson, who is known for his pure aesthetic and process of reduction, once famously said, 'Minimalism is not defined by what is not there but by the rightness of what is and the richness with which this is experienced.' By intentionally reducing your possessions you become more aware of the items you truly cherish, allowing you to focus on the present moment and cultivate a more enriched home and life.

Dealing with clutter can be a daunting task, so the best approach is a slow one. Break down the process into manageable steps and start by focusing on one room or area at a time. If it's a space that is particularly overwhelming – such as a spare room that has become a bit of a dumping ground, start small with a set of drawers or a bookshelf. Clear everything away, allowing the space to breathe. As you strip back the layers and dust surfaces clean, pay attention to the essence of the room. Look for details that may have gone unnoticed before – the play of light on a wall, the beautiful wood grain of a dining table previously buried in books. Identifying characteristics like these that you wish to

celebrate encourages a more intentional approach to deciding what to keep and what will help to shape the space.

Purposefully eliminate excess by asking key questions about each item: Does it serve a practical purpose? Does it bring joy or hold sentimental value? Parting ways with personal belongings can be difficult at first, but soon you will embrace the liberating feeling of letting go. There is nothing quite like experiencing a newly decluttered space to inspire further effort. Decluttering can also be a journey of rediscovery. You might unearth a hidden treasure, see something in a different light or decide to give an object that has seen better days a new lease on life. Remember, it's not about striving for perfection. Items with nostalgic or sentimental value often exhibit imperfections and signs of wear and tear, adding to their charm. Whether it's a chipped ceramic vase, carrying the memories of a loved one, or a vintage lamp full of character, albeit in need of a new shade, these pieces add to the essence of a space - one that is unique to you.

Thoughtful storage

When creating a serene home environment, it's important to acknowledge that not everything warrants being on display. Introducing considered storage solutions is crucial for minimizing clutter, improving organization and maintaining order throughout your interior. When selecting furniture, invest in versatile pieces that include storage. Sideboards, shelving units and bedside tables are all great options, seamlessly blending open shelves with concealed storage compartments. This allows you to showcase cherished items like books, art and ceramics, while discreetly stowing away everyday items that require easy accessibility but contribute to visual clutter, such as television remotes and candle lighters. If you're not able to invest in new furniture, get creative with beautiful baskets that can fit neatly inside existing shelves. When embarking on a building or

renovation project, seize the opportunity to integrate storage solutions into your design. Pay special attention to hardworking spaces like the kitchen, exploring ideas such as an island with shelves for cookbooks and serving dishes, compartmentalized draws to neatly store utensils, a designated area to house and conceal appliances, and integrated bins for recycling. Custom cabinetry and bespoke furniture solutions can extend to every room of the home. Some ideas to consider are built-in window seating with storage in the living room, recessed shelving in bathrooms and customized wardrobe designs for bedrooms. Store off-season items such as knitwear and heavy bed linen during the warmer months. Underbed storage is a great place for this.

Habits and rituals

Decluttering is not a one-off task but rather an ongoing practice that requires consistent attention. Take the time to frequently assess your belongings, considering what still serves a purpose and what no longer resonates with your life or style. By letting go of unnecessary items on a regular basis, you'll maintain a clutter-free home and prevent visual noise from building up. To avoid overwhelm when decluttering, plan ahead so that you know where items are going. Only throw things away when it's absolutely necessary. Many items can be recycled or donated, and there are a growing number of options to ensure unwanted things are put back into the community, rather than ending up in landfills. Create routines that make decluttering a natural part of your day-to-day activities. Incorporate small sessions into your daily schedule, whether it's tidying up a specific area or purging things you no longer need. Assigning a designated place for each item also helps to maintain order and makes it easier to put things away after use. This could be as simple as a bowl on the entrance console for keys and wall hooks for coats. Additionally, set aside dedicated time each season to tackle larger-scale decluttering, and determine what you want to keep, donate or discard. That way you will regularly refresh and streamline your belongings, ensuring you hold on to only what you truly need and cherish.

Considered curation

A beautiful, nuanced home celebrates timelessness rather than fleeting trends and should reflect those who inhabit it, telling the stories of their lives. But how do you curate a home with intentionality - one that feels authentic to you?

In essence, it's about embracing the things you love and gradually adding layers that are uniquely personal. These layers, which can stem from your interests, lifestyle and travels, represent who you are and your diverse experiences and tastes, values, aspirations and knowledge. Your personal attributes are constantly evolving, and they make your home unlike any other. Just as we are distinctly different from one another, so too are our homes. As Rick Rubin says in his book *The Creative Act: A Way of Being*, 'The goal is not to fit in. If anything, it's to amplify the differences, what doesn't fit, the special characteristics unique to how you see the world.'

The process of curating can begin at any stage, following a major renovation, a small-scale update or a simple room declutter. If you are renovating, now is a good time to think about how you will curate the space once the renovation is complete. Honour the architectural roots of your home but keep the overall design pared back and adhere to a neutral colour palette. If the room starts with a strong identity in terms of colour, panelling or artworks hung on every wall, this leaves little leeway for curating now or in the future. Remember, our homes need space to evolve with us. Regardless of whether that home is newly built, renovated or just as we have found it, it should be one that we can grow into.

Whether you are starting from scratch or adding to existing pieces, begin by taking everything out of the room, leaving a neutral, airy space. Allow the natural light and architecture to breathe. Consider how the room feels in its rawest form, what original features speak to you and how these can be celebrated. Place furniture you wish to keep and let these pieces inform what is missing, without the need to fill the space. These things don't need to be expensive - in fact, a mix of high- and low-end pieces will create much more interest. Adhere to your overall colour

KINFOLK
ARRANGING THINGS
SOFT MINIMAL

scheme - with neutral tones as your canvas - and add depth with texture and pattern. Blend old and new, look for handcrafted and one-of-a-kind objects and always inject your personality. Just as decluttering is a gradual process, so too should be the accumulation of items. A quiet, considered home is never rushed; it allows for research and fine-tuning. Being mindful and present during this process will ensure that the path to curating a quiet home is enjoyable. A slow and purposeful curation of pieces that reflect your way of life will ultimately lead to a home that isn't just for show but one that you and those you choose to spend your life with enjoy being in. This is a home that beckons you to touch and discover, to walk through it, to sit and to fully experience it - a sanctuary that feels welcoming, warm, comfortable and safe, and truly represents you and your family.

If you come across an interior space - in a magazine, online or in real life - that resonates strongly with you, think about how it makes you feel and why it evokes an emotive response. Is it the light, the way the pieces are styled or a combination of certain textures? Don't focus on replicating a 'look' but rather on identifying why it makes you feel a certain way. Through this process of digging a little deeper, you can start to uncover what speaks to you so that you can make more intuitive decisions when it comes to choosing your own pieces without losing sight of your overall goal - to create a home that reflects you and what you love, with a mix of objects sourced from different places over the course of your life.

Curating a considered home

Embrace a slow accumulation

Take your time to ensure that each addition – from furniture and lighting to art and smaller objects – is intentional, well thought-out and enhances your overall space. Be patient and make discerning choices. Don't be tempted by a quick fix if you can't immediately find what you are looking for, must wait for availability or long manufacturing times, or need to save up for something special. The time spent waiting will be brief compared to the lasting presence of a carefully chosen forever piece.

Experiment

Approach the curation of your home with curiosity and an open mind. Minimalist homes aren't about being safe or following what's fashionable. Push the boundaries of your own creativity and experiment with different things: use an incense holder as a vase to display a single dried stem, showcase a book on your coffee table open to a favourite page with a beautiful bookmark or display something on your wall that wasn't intended as artwork, such as a ceramic platter or a tapestry blanket. These elements of surprise contribute to the overall magic.

Enjoy the journey

Create mood boards (digital or physical) with inspirational images, colour schemes, materials and textures. Look beyond obvious sources like social media and magazines. Interior inspiration can come from anywhere – books, films, travel, fashion or the arts. Be an observer, and view curation as a way of life. Make decisions on new purchases with care: research thoroughly; measure your space; test fabric, material and paint swatches in your home; and, if necessary, view furniture in your home before you place an order.

Collect meaningful items

Celebrate the handcrafted with thoughtful objects that keep ancient skills and practices alive. Focus on items that ignite feelings of nostalgia, carry memories and remind you of significant moments in your life, such as travel souvenirs, artworks, heirlooms or treasured books. Pieces with meaning don't need to cost the earth. They can be as simple as shells or stones collected from a beautiful beach you visited or a framed piece of your child's artwork.

Blend old and new

Don't be afraid to combine pieces from different periods. Traditional and contemporary styles can coexist, and when combined thoughtfully, they inject charm and character into your home. The key to blending a mix of eras is to look for common design elements, such as materials, colour tones, proportions and shapes, and to play off contrasts like straight edges with rounded forms. This approach will help you create a harmonious and cohesive feel. For example, in your living room, you might pair a modern, linear bookshelf with a curved vintage sofa. The warm wood of the shelves could then carry through to a secondhand wooden coffee table, while the stone finish of a contemporary side table might be echoed by an antique travertine sculpture on the shelves.

Widen your search

We all have our favourite stores and haunts, but rather than looking in the same places or revisiting online shops, broaden your search. Keep an eye out for auctions and vintage treasures; visit local antique stores, charity shops and flea markets; and do the same when you are travelling. Those off-the-beaten-track places are often where you will uncover special gems.

The passage of time

Mindful minimalism is about choosing well and finding beauty in honest and enduring design. In a world filled with increasing online noise, this approach can be hindered by an algorithm-fuelled stream of sameness that leaves you fatigued and overwhelmed. Online shopping can also heighten the temptation to make impulse purchases of hastily designed, cheaply made items that can be delivered to your door in days. This can lead to dissatisfaction and the continual need to replace items that quickly wear out or lose their appeal – a cycle that contributes to a throwaway culture and the accumulation of unwanted clutter. So, how do you break this pattern and create lasting change? Often, the way forward is found by looking to the past.

The interior design world has always sought inspiration from bygone eras, continually reinventing ideas from previous periods. This practice stems from our innate need to connect with the past and the stories it tells, creating a sense of history in the spaces we inhabit. This connection is also about the human aspect of design and is why we are continually drawn to historic pieces when creating meaningful, layered interiors. Take Hans Wegner's Wishbone chair, for example. You can feel the craftsmanship in its iconic curves, made from a single piece of solid, steam-bent wood, and its expertly hand-woven paper cord seat. Or consider Georg Jensen's strikingly elegant Koppel pitcher. A masterpiece of mid-century modern Scandinavian design, its timeless, minimal shape and stainless steel finish feels as contemporary today as it did when it was originally created by sculptor Henning Koppel in 1952.

When you encounter something well-designed and beautifully made with human touches it evokes emotion. We crave that connection to the past because such pieces offer longevity, comfort and a story. Historic and enduring items ground us, providing solace in a world that often feels temporary and disposable.

You don't need to be an expert on the history of design, but understanding different periods can give your interior project context and help guide you when making decisions, from the broader aspects

of spatial design through to choosing finishes like flooring and tiles, as well as sourcing furniture and decorative pieces. Knowing the architectural period of your home, for instance, can guide your renovation, revealing what has been covered up or removed in previous updates. While seeking to improve the layout for increased function and liveability, you can look at restoring and accentuating original architectural details to maintain the sense of history, character and charm of a space.

Consider a century-old Californian bungalow undergoing a reworking of its existing heritage footprint with a modern extension at the rear. This project requires innovative spatial planning and a cohesive colour palette to seamlessly connect the old and the new. The final result should create a sense that the past gently overlaps with the present, and the extension feels like an evolution rather than a modern add-on.

Similarly, the architectural details of a Victorian villa can be reinvigorated and juxtaposed with contemporary ideas of space, light and material expression. For example, intricate plasterwork on ceiling cornices and arched doorways could be restored and accompanied by contemporary wooden flooring and tiling. On a simpler scale, heritage features such as original mouldings, mantles and fire surrounds can be maintained but updated with a fresh coat of paint in a neutral shade, creating a more modern, airy feel.

Whether you are carrying out significant interventions or a smaller-scale refresh, avoid becoming a slave to the original home and resist the urge to replicate it. Instead, renovate sensitively by celebrating the essence of the house while adding your unique touch. Look backwards but also look forwards. By thoughtfully blending the past, present and future, you honour the timeless elements that define a space while ensuring it resonates with both history and contemporary life.

Over time, as your needs shift and your life evolves, these layers become richer, allowing the home to grow with you – acquiring depth, meaning and familiarity.

The beauty of age

Calming spaces are restful, but they are also uplifting. A crucial aspect of bringing life to minimalist interiors is introducing elements that add texture and warmth - qualities inherently found in aged and timeworn pieces. Whether it's an architectural feature such as weathered wooden beams or a decorative element like an antique metal sculpture, their allure lies in their ability to inject contrast into a space - offsetting clean with rustic, smooth with rough, and shiny with matte. Natural, honest materials such as wood, stone and leather develop distinctive patinas, testifying to the passage of time and the stories embedded within.

Celebrating flaws that occur naturally with age and the ephemeral aspect of life is part of the Japanese philosophy of *wabi-sabi*. When applied to interiors, this translates to an appreciation for the history told through different textures and surfaces - such as scratches on a dining table that has been passed down through generations, telling the story of countless family gatherings and celebrations, or the uneven glaze of a ceramic vase which only adds to its unique charm. By embracing these natural, aged imperfections, you will create textural variation and depth, imbuing spaces with a sensorial, lived-in feel.

Sustainable, enduring materials such as timber, stone, bamboo, cork and clay are beautifully tactile with organic irregularity, and will ground your interiors in nature, enhancing the authenticity and warmth of the spaces. When deciding on a piece of furniture or an object for your home, think about how it will look in five years' time, and how you will feel about it. Choose well-made pieces that combine form and function. Honest design and quality craftsmanship will always stand the test of time.

If you love the idea of buying secondhand but feel intimidated or overwhelmed, start with something small like a wooden stool or a light fixture. You'll be surprised by the impact it can create, whether enhancing traditional architecture or adding an unexpected element to a contemporary home. Keep an open mind when viewing pieces that are looking tired or shabby. New upholstery can completely transform a sofa or armchair. A dated bookshelf with great bones, or an inherited vintage sideboard, can be invigorated when stripped back and refinished. Always restore with respect: not all finds need to be preserved in the state you found them, but be careful not to strip something of its original detailing or cover up a patina-rich surface at the expense of erasing history, authenticity and charm.

JAPANESE

Quiet luxury

In the context of home, quiet luxury is felt as much as it is seen. Expressed through restraint and discernment rather than excess or embellishment, the focus is on a respect for craftsmanship, authenticity and lasting quality. Materials are selected not only for their beauty, but for the skill and tradition behind their making. Meticulously crafted joinery, hand-finished stone and custom upholstery speak to a level of care that elevates the everyday. A muted palette of natural finishes carries effortlessly from one room to the next, creating a refined sense of cohesion. These spaces don't shout for attention; instead, they radiate quiet confidence - elegant, understated and enduring.

A relaxed refinement

A common misconception around minimalist interiors is that they are sparse and uninviting, and that they aren't conducive to family life or relaxation. While a minimalist approach will lead to clean and refined spaces, it should never be about sacrificing comfort and cosiness. In fact, finding the perfect balance between simplicity and warmth is at the heart of quiet luxury. How you go about achieving that balance has a lot to do with layering and the use of natural materials, offsetting smooth and textured surfaces and paying attention to fine detailing. Indeed, quiet luxury goes hand in hand with a subdued colour palette, but regardless of your home's style - contemporary or traditional - the same principles when applied to either will create a cosy tranquillity.

Authenticity, another key characteristic, is achieved by celebrating a home's existing strengths, such as architectural elements or a connection to the outdoors. Any updates should be carried out with respect for the building's history and its environment, using materials that blend with the home's existing fabric and surrounding landscape. For example, a home located near the coastline could echo the nearby dunes with curvy textured walls in sandy tones, pale wood flooring and softly veined

travertine benchtops. Alternatively, original oak flooring could be left raw and unpolished during the restoration process and a concrete kitchen island installed to mimic the rugged terrain. Subtle layers of tactile and tonally balanced colours woven throughout will add depth while also uniting spaces through a commonality. At the centre of quiet luxury's celebration of enduring materials is a commitment to sustainability. Where possible, use locally sourced or reclaimed materials and eco-friendly solutions.

Quiet luxury manifests in the tactile pleasures of daily life: a sumptuous rug underfoot, handcrafted by skilled artisans; the gentle softness of sheer curtains allowing ethereal light to filter through; the textured nuances of limewashed walls. Even the smallest details, such as the handles you choose for wardrobe doors, can contribute to the narrative of your home, imbuing it with serenity and charm. Materiality plays a pivotal role, drawing inspiration from nature to incorporate tactile surfaces like wood and stone. Combining two key materials, such as a rich, dark wood and luxurious marble, will create an interplay of textures to add depth and interest. Continuing this pairing throughout the home will provide a feeling of unity, cultivating a contrasting yet cohesive environment. To further enhance the tactile experience of the space, soften hard surfaces with textiles crafted from natural fibres such as linen and wool, and incorporate tactility into artworks. Inject sensory elements that appeal not only to sight and touch but also to smell, like fragrant flowers and scented candles. In this way you'll create spaces to savour and engage with every day, and for years to come.

Light and dark

We've established the importance of natural light, and ways to harness its power for improved wellness. But darkness and shadows, which are inextricably linked to light, are equally important in the perception and experience of space. Without areas of darkness, light would fail to create impact and spaces would simply appear flat and one-dimensional.

Light and shadow work together to bring textures to life. Throughout the day, sunlight interacts with surfaces in ever-changing ways - casting patterns, softening edges and highlighting details. The way shadows fall across furniture, the gentle gradation of light on a wall or a glint of sunlight on the edge of a stone benchtop can subtly alter the energy of a room.

Much like when we look at a painting, where light and shadow are fundamental elements – the driving force of the technique of chiaroscuro, derived from the Italian words meaning 'light' and 'dark', and established during the Renaissance by Leonardo da Vinci and Caravaggio – it's contrast that provides effect and engages our senses. Leonardo worked light and shadow into his brooding, atmospheric paintings to give a vivid three-dimensionality to his figures, and Caravaggio, the master of theatricality, used such contrasts for the sake of drama. Both artists knew how emotionally arresting these effects were.

Similarly, our homes can take us on a journey through brightness and shade as we move through different areas. For example, a light-filled entranceway leading to a darker, moodier front living room creates a dynamic contrast, emphasizing the specific function of each area. The entrance provides a welcoming glow, while the living room provides a cocoon-like feel for quiet moments of solitude or intimate social gatherings. A dark hallway creates a moment of mystery as it leads to a large and airy living space at the back of the house. Imagine feeling the sense of spaciousness as the open-plan area reveals itself with vaulted ceilings, clerestory windows and a flood of natural light. Bedrooms may purposely be painted in a darker hue to create a cosy, enveloping feel, while a bathroom skylight placed above a freestanding bath invites tranquil spa-like moments. Within a room, light and shadow also create poetry: for example, natural light streaming through a large window on one wall and a dark, textural artwork on another. Through their duality, interplay and rhythm, light and dark give a space its sense of both scale and intimacy, revealing nuances of materials, volumes and forms. As Japanese novelist Junichiro Tanizaki said in his enchanting essay *In Praise of Shadows*, 'we find beauty not in the thing itself but in the patterns of shadows, the light and the darkness, that one thing against another creates...Were it not for shadows, there would be no beauty.'

Quiet luxury may be a lesson in restraint, but it is rich with the atmospheric beauty found in everyday moments such as light filtering through tree branches and shadows dancing on textured interior walls. This becomes more apparent as we experience the change of seasons in our homes. Witnessing the variations in the strength and intensity of light and shadow throughout the year deepens our emotional connection with our surroundings and enhances our overall sense of well-being.

Slow living

Imagine creating a home where, upon entry, the outside world fades away with each step - where the speed of life slows and is replaced by a sense of tranquillity and introspection. The quiet home does just this - it invites a slower pace, providing time to pause and reflect. It begins with minimalist interiors, which offer the ideal backdrop for slow living and appreciating the beauty of simplicity. When the spaces you live in are uncluttered and calm, your mind can also find peace, allowing you to be fully present in the moment. However, a home that supports slow living isn't just about minimalism or adhering to a particular style; it involves fostering a holistic approach to ensure that the spaces are not only visually pleasing but also functional and emotionally resonant, reflecting the values of those who live in them while also nurturing their health and well-being. It's a home that deepens awareness, encourages intentionality and celebrates sustainability.

Holistic interiors

A holistic approach considers the whole of something, rather than just its parts. In terms of interiors, it encompasses the sustainability of materials, the amount of light, the quality of air, the sense of calm created by the interplay of design elements and the connection to nature. It also emphasizes human-centric design, focusing on the needs of those who use the space, and balancing areas for both social interaction and personal solace. Holistic spaces begin with a mindful material palette that celebrates natural, organic and sustainable choices, contributing to a healthier living environment. This approach encourages us to ask critical questions from the outset. How is a product is made? Who made it? Where should it be used?

Design choices that foster holistic harmony and balance enhance both our homes and our lives. They include all elements, from building materials and colour palettes to textiles, furniture and finishing touches.

Slow interiors favour elements such as muted colours, softly flowing fabrics and unobtrusive, functional furniture. By setting the tone for a graceful ambience that cultivates tranquillity, they naturally encourage a deceleration of day-to-day life. So often, we operate on autopilot, constantly thinking about the next task. Calm spaces allow us to decompress, switch to a more present state of mind and transform daily tasks into purposeful rituals and simple moments into indulgent experiences. This might be savouring your morning coffee from a cherished handmade ceramic mug, curling up on your favourite sofa with a loved one on a peaceful Sunday morning, or lighting warming candles in the evening with dinner.

Connection with nature

Slow living encourages us to rethink our perspectives on time and the pace at which we live, work and consume. It's not just about slowing down our daily routines; it's about deepening our connections with ourselves, each other and our environment, including the natural world. Reconnecting with nature is fundamental to slow living because it draws us away from our increasingly fast-paced lives and puts us back in touch with the natural rhythm of the world around us.

Time spent outdoors is restorative, offering significant benefits for both our mental and physical health. Embracing the cycle of changing seasons - such as watching the leaves change colour and daylight hours shift - promotes mindfulness. This practice helps us slow down, feel grounded and find balance, making it essential for our homes to connect with nature. Matt Gibberd, founding director of UK estate agency The Modern House, emphasizes this in his book *A Modern Way to Live*: 'If you are on the lookout for a new home, a connection to nature should be the first thing on your wish list, regardless of budget.'

Fostering this connection involves creating a continuous dialogue between indoor and outdoor spaces. This starts with a visual link to the outdoors, which, depending on your home and location, could range from a small garden or balcony to expansive countryside views. If space is limited, consider placing potted plants or trees by windows, or growing herbs and flowers in balcony boxes. For more spacious areas, extending living spaces outdoors is a wonderful way to enhance your connection with nature. This encourages spending time outdoors during moments

of solitude, with family for regular meals and activities or when entertaining friends. Crafting a seamless indoor-outdoor flow is the next step, which extends beyond the visual; it's about forging a harmonious living experience that merges the built and natural environments.

There are many ways to enhance this connection to create harmony between interior and exterior living areas. Harnessing natural light and garden views will foster relaxation within open spaces that carry through to the outdoor areas. If you are renovating, invest in landscaping. It looks beautiful and cannot be underestimated when it comes to increasing the functionality of your home. It also helps to create a sound barrier on noisy roads and enhances privacy. If you're at the planning stage of a design, consider the positioning of windows, doors and access routes, all of which are integral to creating seamless transitions. As well as determining what will suit you and your outdoor area, you'll learn how to deal with ongoing garden maintenance such as pruning, watering and seasonal care. To encourage biodiversity, select native plants that support local wildlife, implement composting and rainwater-harvesting systems to reduce waste and conserve water and integrate water features to create a tranquil outdoor atmosphere.

Prioritizing sustainable materials that blend with the landscape is also important, as is creating cohesion through colour palettes and finishes. As renowned architect Tadao Ando said, 'We borrow from nature the space upon which we build.' Carefully chosen surface finishes will develop a natural patina and soften boundaries, strengthening the connection between your home and its surroundings.

When it comes to furnishings, treat exterior spaces like interior ones by creating serene areas for rest and relaxation. Focus on comfort and adaptability for different uses and allow for the space to evolve with you and your family over time. All these elements not only enhance the aesthetics of outdoor areas but also improve functionality and create a calming ambience, transforming gardens, terraces and balconies into true extensions of your indoor living spaces.

Blending interior and exterior living spaces

Extend sightlines
Focus on extending living and dining areas to outdoor terraces or gardens. If you're in the design stage, carefully plan sightlines. Large windows and doors not only allow natural light into your home but also frame garden views and create focal points that draw the eye towards the outdoor landscape. Consider all areas of the home to maximize its potential beyond the interior experience. Additionally, lean into a neutral interior palette to allow the lush greenery of nature to radiate through.

Create seamless transitions
Extend flooring materials like wood or tiles to exterior spaces to blur transition lines and organically merge inside and out. Ceiling continuity will also help create a seamless transition and natural flow. For example, extend ceiling beams, tiles or wood panelling to a covered deck or patio. Use the same stone or brick in exterior walls to build planters, fireplaces or built-in barbecue areas, and water features. To add shelter and privacy without feeling too enclosed, consider using side walls and flexible solutions like moveable screens or louvres.

Foster sustainability
Create outdoor living spaces that blend with the landscape and respect the existing natural elements. Use sustainable materials that offer long-term durability, such as FSC-certified wood, bamboo and stone. Incorporate reclaimed wood in structures like walls, fences, decks and patios. Reclaimed bricks, stones or tiles can also be used to build retaining walls and pave walkways.

Incorporate lighting
Landscape lighting blurs the borders between inside and out, allowing you to enjoy the beauty of the entire space. When creating an outdoor lighting plan, consider the areas you want to illuminate, such as pathways, a barbecue area or specific features of your garden, and the level of brightness you want to achieve. This will help guide you through a myriad of choices, including dimmable and solar-powered options, ground-level spotlights, wall-mounted or hanging lights and portable LED lamps. Choose designs that complement your home's aesthetic and blend with the natural environment to enhance the overall harmony and continuity.

Choose complementary furnishings

To create outdoor areas that feel like an extension of your interior living space, choose furniture and décor that complement the interior scheme. Implement similar tones and textures and select versatile pieces that cater to different activities - enjoying a morning coffee, dining alfresco with the family or hosting a gathering with friends. FSC-certified teak is a great option for its sustainability and ability to withstand outdoor conditions. Use weather-resistant rugs, sectional sofas, chairs, side tables and ottomans to create adaptable, inviting and functional exterior living spaces.

Use landscaping

The landscape serves as more than just a backdrop; it's an active player in unifying indoor and outdoor spaces. Choose native plants that thrive in your region and carefully plan the placement of plants, trees and hardscaping to extend visual continuity. Incorporating water features, garden paths and other elements that draw the eye outward encourages exploration and interaction with the outdoor space, enriching the overall living experience.

Chapter three

The art of the edit

Crafting a quiet and tranquil home requires careful editing. Removing things can significantly impact the look and feel of your interiors, but editing an interior space involves more than mere subtraction. It's a process of fine-tuning and introducing layers to create balance and harmony. It requires the ability to view the space in its entirety, while also paying attention to smaller details – such as cushions, books, sculptural ceramics and art – and how they are styled. Editing is an ongoing practice. Embracing change and regularly rearranging areas of your home will keep spaces feeling fresh and interesting. Even shuffling books and objects on the coffee table or shelves and adding some fresh flowers can make a big difference. Over time, editing will become more instinctive and even habitual – an enjoyable and rewarding process.

The following methods for editing a space can be applied to different interior styles, such as Scandinavian or mid-century modern, and to homes from different eras, from heritage properties to contemporary. Tapping into your own personal style will ensure your home is truly authentic, and from here, you can apply the strategies outlined in this chapter, including leveraging principles of design such as proportion, scale and composition, and employing styling techniques that embrace the beauty of negative space. Each approach is underpinned by the ethos that calming interiors refrain from overstyling and nurture subtle signs of life, creating an atmosphere of relaxed elegance that invites tranquillity into every corner.

Proportion and scale

When styling your home, choosing the right proportions and scale for each element go a long way in creating quiet and harmonious spaces. The pieces you select should feel as though they belong, forming a subtle dialogue with each other to foster a sense of balance and cohesion. As the world-renowned French interior designer Andrée Putman once said, 'For a house to be successful, the objects in it must communicate with one another, respond and balance one another.'

Achieving this flow begins with understanding proportion and scale - and how to apply them throughout your home. Proportion relates to how objects compare in size to one another, while scale considers their size in relation to the room itself. As well as size, architectural elements, like ceiling height, significantly impact how a room feels. Lower ceilings create intimacy, while higher ones expand the space.

As you select furniture, keep the room size in mind. Large pieces in small spaces can feel cramped, but too many small pieces can make the area feel equally cluttered. Conversely, small furniture in a large room can be easily lost. Opting for fewer, larger statement pieces - an oversized artwork or a mirror - can enhance a room's spaciousness. Floor rugs, too, play a significant role: a rug that fills the floor will anchor the space, while one too small can disrupt the balance.

In larger spaces, create focal points with a hero piece, such as a sofa, then build smaller elements around it that harmonize with its scale. Repeating shapes and patterns in varying sizes fosters visual unity, while grouping individual pieces together can tell a cohesive story. In open-plan areas, furniture should fill the space naturally, never overpowering it. Mirrors or tall bookshelves can balance vertical spaces, while layered lighting can bring focus to certain areas, enhancing intimacy.

In interiors, visual weight isn't a measure of an object's physical heaviness but rather how it appears to the eye - a perception shaped by size, colour, shape, texture and placement. When you enter a room that feels just right, it's because the visual weight has been distributed in a harmonious way, maintaining equilibrium and providing a sense of calm.

Francis Bacon
LOST BUILDINGS
THE TOUCH

Balancing visual weight in the home

Harness scale and proportion

Visual weight influences how we perceive scale and proportion in a room. A large, dark piece of furniture might anchor the space, creating a sense of gravitas, while smaller, lighter elements introduce contrast and soften the overall feel. This interplay affects the room's mood: lighter tones and airy designs evoke openness and tranquillity, while darker hues and more substantial forms bring intimacy and depth. By understanding this balance, you can shape the overall feel of your home, ensuring each room reflects the mood you want to create.

Introduce texture and shape

Texture plays a vital role in adding richness and substance to a room. Coarse, textured materials – such as a woven rug, a chunky knit throw or a reclaimed wood table – feel visually heavier than smooth or glossy surfaces. Incorporating textures thoughtfully can add warmth and interest without overwhelming the space. Similarly, shape affects how objects are perceived. Rounded edges, like those on circular mirrors or oval tables, tend to feel lighter and more fluid, compared to angular designs. Combining soft, rounded forms with clean, linear pieces creates a sense of balance, allowing each element to complement the other.

Develop your palette

Colour is one of the most powerful tools for influencing visual weight. Dark, saturated or warm hues feel heavier, grounding the room and drawing the eye, while lighter tones recede, creating a softer, more subdued effect. To foster a quiet, harmonious atmosphere, choose a palette of gentle hues with similar undertones to create cohesion and flow. For an open, airy feel, prioritize lighter shades, using darker tones sparingly as accents to maintain a sense of lightness. For a moodier, cosier ambience, use deeper hues as a backdrop, balanced by lighter elements to prevent the space from feeling too heavy. Every choice – from paint colours and fabrics to furniture and art – should be considered based on how it interacts with the surrounding elements. A thoughtfully chosen palette ensures the space feels connected, soothing and intentional.

Create strategic details

Even the smallest details contribute to balance. Thoughtful vignettes – a stack of books paired with a vase on coffee table, or a grouping of objects on a sideboard – create moments of intentionality. The goal is to avoid any area feeling overly heavy or light, allowing the eye to roam effortlessly through the space.

Distribute elements evenly

Balance is achieved by distributing visual weight evenly. Larger, heavier pieces - a dark sofa or a statement dining table - ground the space, while lighter elements, like soft textiles, airy pendant lights, small objects or curated groupings, provide contrast. Mixing elements - vintage with modern, curved with linear, hard with soft - creates dynamic spaces that feel both calming and unique. Incorporating pieces of varying sizes, shapes and heights encourages the gaze to move naturally, creating a sense of flow and synergy.

Take your time

Creating a balanced home is a gradual process. After moving, renovating or decluttering, resist the urge to rush and allow each space to evolve naturally. Taking your time gives you the chance to curate pieces that truly resonate with you, layering them thoughtfully to create a home that feels personal, harmonious and reflective of your style. This slow, intentional approach results in spaces that are not only balanced but also nurturing to your well-being - a true expression of the quiet home concept.

Composition

Composition in interior design is the subtle art of arranging elements to create a spatial flow that balances movement and stillness within a larger narrative. But creating harmonious arrangements throughout the home extends well beyond the selection and placement of furniture. While these are significant steps in the process, the fine details and delicate nuances found in shelf displays and sideboard vignettes are as important as hero pieces such as a sofa or floor lamp. In fact, these smaller compositions are what elevate interior styling to an art form, providing each space with a sense of warmth and character and, ultimately, transforming a house into a cherished home.

The impact of art

Art is an essential element of composition, bringing richness, texture and a sense of individuality to a space. It creates focal points that draw the eye and add contrast, whether you choose a single statement piece above the sofa, a quiet and understated work in the bedroom or a carefully curated gallery wall in the hallway.

By introducing rhythm and balance, a piece of art can set the tone for an entire space or serve as the finishing touch that completes a room. It might add subtle colour and contrast or bring dimension to minimal interiors – enhancing the mood without overwhelming it.

But art isn't just decorative – it's deeply emotive. A piece of art can evoke memories, inspire a feeling or provide comfort. Art invites us to see the world through new perspectives, enriching our lives in unexpected ways. Through the process of thoughtfully selecting and placing art, you will make your home feel personal and layered – a reflection of who you are, offering warmth, character and a quiet sense of connection.

The building blocks of composition

A focal point

A focal point is what captures the eye when you enter a room. It might be a statement artwork in the living room or, on a smaller scale, a floral arrangement on a dining-room sideboard. Regardless of what it is, it should be something that captivates and makes your heart sing. It can also be used as a guide for selecting other pieces in relation to colour, texture or form. A favourite hue, shape or pattern from the focal point could be echoed in other pieces such as cushions, ceramics or rugs. This will create cohesion throughout the composition and your home.

Variation

Avoid confusing cohesion with sameness by sourcing pieces all from the same store or trying to create uniform arrangements in every space. This will quickly lead to a humdrum repetitiveness. Carry similar themes throughout your spaces, such as colour tones, shapes and materials, but at the same time inject variety by curating objects with differing heights, contrasting texture and patterns, and pieces that reflect your personal style. These variations guide the eye around a composition, as we instinctively focus on where objects start and finish, and areas of convergence or overlap. Also play with asymmetry. Just as there is beauty in imperfection, there is magic to be found in irregularity and the unexpected.

A composed coffee table

A key element of any living room, the coffee table is as much about function as it is about aesthetics. Usually placed centrally, it grounds and enhances the overall space. As well as keeping your cup of coffee or reading material in easy reach, the table provides an opportunity to showcase things you love, such as books on interior design with beautiful covers or sculptural ceramics, and to inject sensory appeal through tactile objects. Let the shape of your table guide you. If it's rectangular or square, create a grouping near the middle, such as a tray, a vase and a candle. Around this, arrange books in a formation of low stacks, paying attention to the sizes and colours to create cohesion. Dot smaller accent pieces on top of the books in an organic style, with a focus on rounded forms to soften the straight lines. These could be as simple as a textural stone, found at the seashore, or a small wooden vessel.

Curated shelves

Shelves not only keep clutter at bay by accommodating everything from books and objects in living spaces through to crockery in the kitchen - they also provide space for you to create beautiful displays. Whether you are styling a single floating shelf or a large modular shelving system, colour cohesion and artful groupings will help radiate a sense of calm. Choose neutral colours with varying subtleties in tones and introduce some dark accents for contrast. Black and chocolate-brown hues pair beautifully with warm neutrals. Place pieces in front and to the side of your focal point to create depth. Odd numbers are inherently more pleasing to the eye, and often just three pieces grouped together will be enough to create impact. Avoid overcrowding by leaving some space between the groupings, and remember to play with different textures and heights. For a unified look, stack your books according to colour and size, but ensure there is some variation, such as larger books graduating to smaller books and dark-coloured spines graduating to lighter ones.

Selecting art with purpose

When selecting pieces, consider how they make you feel. Do they evoke a memory, bring enjoyment or create a sense of calm? The right choice will resonate emotionally and complement the aesthetic of your space.

You might choose a vintage still-life painting to enhance the intimacy of a dining room or a soothing landscape or abstract work with muted tones to create serenity in a bedroom. A home near the coast might feature seascapes, while a forest retreat could incorporate artwork inspired by trees. Beyond aesthetics, think about how the art integrates into the story of your home and its surroundings.

Size, too, plays a crucial role. Large-scale pieces can dominate and create impact, but smaller works often captivate in intimate ways. A diminutive, intriguing artwork can create a dynamic essence, inviting closer inspection and offering an unexpected moment of delight.

Thoughtful placement

Art placement can transform how a room feels, and it requires thoughtful consideration. Think about overall harmony of the space: will the piece create a focal point, anchor the room or contribute to visual balance? In some cases, leaving a wall bare allows the room to breathe, while in others, a carefully placed artwork ties elements together. In transitional areas like hallways, consider how a piece engages both from afar and up close. Above a sofa, ensure the size and positioning of artworks resonates with the scale of the room.

It's also important to consider light and framing. To prevent fading, avoid placing art in direct sunlight. Use anti-reflective glass to reduce reflections, and adjust the angle of your room lighting to minimize glare. You might also explore frameless pieces or sculpture.

Unconventional arrangements can add a sense of playfulness and creativity. Try hanging two artworks asymmetrically or at varying heights to create a dynamic effect. For gallery walls, cut paper templates of your artwork and test different configurations before committing. Be sure to leave enough space between pieces to avoid a cluttered appearance.

Art doesn't always need to be fixed in place. Leaning artworks on a fireplace mantel, shelves or a sideboard offers flexibility and creative freedom, making it easy to refresh your space regularly.

LIVE BEAUTIFUL

Breathing space

In interiors, the balance between positive and negative space is achieved in much the same way as an artist composes a canvas - by purposefully leaving areas devoid of colour or detail, attention is naturally drawn to what remains. Positive space encompasses furniture, décor and architectural elements - the visible, tangible features that ground and define a room. Negative space, often overlooked, is the air around elements that lets a room breathe: the open floor, the unoccupied walls and the spaces between objects. Together, positive and negative space create balance and harmony throughout the home.

Embracing the beauty of negative space fosters a quiet, minimalist interior. The deliberate use of empty space highlights key elements, creates flow and offers the eye a place to rest. Used intentionally, it is a powerful tool in the quiet home, cutting through visual noise to provide depth and dimension. Negative space gives every object room to resonate, while the spaces between act as pauses in conversation - a moment to stop and breathe.

The importance of the void

In Chinese classical painting, empty space, known as *xu*, is seen as an essential element of a composition. Painters masterfully employ open spaces to evoke emotions and invite the mind to wander, offering stillness and moments for quiet reflection, fostering a connection that extends beyond the visible. In the quiet home, the concept of the void speaks to our own need for breathing space - an intentional clearing that makes room for tranquillity and the beauty of what remains.

Negative space has a profound impact on how a room feels and functions. More than just empty area, it enhances light, facilitates easy movement and makes the room more comfortable and accessible. Each room's scale, proportions and layout will influence how much space can be left open. It's not about following a formula but about tuning into

the room's needs and rhythms. In spaces designed for relaxation, such as living rooms and bedrooms, negative space promotes calm and emotional well-being, minimizing stress and enhancing our sense of ease.

Open areas also enhance focus, making spaces more functional for activities like work or study by reducing visual distractions. In smaller spaces, negative space can even create an illusion of openness, fostering a sense of spaciousness that feels airy and uncluttered.

Framing and flow

Begin by carrying out a full assessment of your space. Identify areas that feel cluttered and remove everything to reveal the room's true proportions - light and architecture flourish when given room to breathe. By understanding the architectural elements and layout of your home, you can apply artistic framing, a design tool that uses negative space to highlight key features such as high ceilings, large windows or a statement fireplace. Just as in a gallery, where blank walls give art room to make an impact, negative space around a feature lets it take centre stage, creating moments of intentional focus within a room.

As you consider the elements you wish to celebrate - perhaps a hero piece of furniture, an architectural detail or a focal artwork - leave ample space around these elements to draw attention, giving them presence and creating visual depth. This understated elegance, created by restraint, allows the beauty of each piece to resonate more fully.

Breathing space goes beyond aesthetics; it affects how we move and interact within a room. Well-considered negative space eases foot traffic, allowing for free, unobstructed movement and reducing visual clutter. In smaller rooms, negative space can even create the illusion of a larger, more open environment, enhancing a sense of scale.

In areas that accommodate multiple activities, such as open-plan living spaces, allow ample space for movement. Divide the room into distinct zones, ensuring that each has breathing space and doesn't encroach upon another. This adds clarity and ease to the flow. When reintroducing furniture, consider placement carefully to achieve balance without overcrowding. Keep only what enhances the space, curating with restraint so that every piece complements the next. Experiment with different arrangements to find the best balance, adjusting or removing pieces until each item feels in harmony with its surroundings.

Rather than following conventional arrangements, ask whether each item truly serves the space. Sometimes, eliminating a central coffee table in favour of small tables alongside seating can create a clearer sightline to a beautiful fireplace or expansive window view. By reimagining traditional layouts you can potentially free up space while redefining the room's functionality. In living rooms, where we unwind, breathing space nurtures well-being by minimizing sensory overload and promoting relaxation.

Another option for maintaining uninterrupted views and open floor space is wall-mounted or low-level furniture. Built-in or recessed shelving, for example, is elegant yet unobtrusive, freeing up space and keeping the room airy. Aim for pieces that speak to each other quietly rather than competing for attention - styling that invites rather than demands.

In the kitchen, embracing negative space might mean leaving certain walls bare, avoiding excessive or hard-to-reach overhead cabinets, and allowing light to open up the room. Rather than converting a light-filled corner into a study nook, you could leave the window unobstructed, allowing natural light to filter through the space. Negative space in the bedroom can help create a restful atmosphere. For instance, you could leave the wall above the headboard bare to direct attention to the bedding's calming textures and colours.

Negative space is a design choice that fosters comfort, peace and freedom, removing the unnecessary to give each room the chance to breathe. In areas where there is pattern, such as in bathroom tiling, think about how you can create pauses: consider using smaller tiles in the shower and larger tiles for the flooring and walls. Install a frameless glass shower for clean, open lines. Negative space here can also mean fewer distractions - an area of simplicity where relaxation and privacy are key.

The choreography of space

A well-balanced room sees its elements in conversation rather than competition. Like a carefully choreographed dance, furniture and décor interact harmoniously with one another, each having their moment to shine. Through artful placement of elements, a room finds rhythm and balance. Small items can be grouped at varying heights, with different textures and shapes, each to contributing to a graceful arrangement. The interaction between objects and spaces invites a natural flow, resulting in a room that feels thoughtfully crafted and intentionally calming.

Poetry in motion

The essence of a home lies in how it makes us feel - a connection shaped by the flow of light, form and energy. When movement is woven into design, it brings a space to life, creating moments that engage both the eye and the soul. This isn't about physical motion but rather the subtle energy created by the interplay of elements - light and shadow, balance and asymmetry, rhythm and stillness. The art lies in the contrasts: dynamic expression tempered by calm, a vibrant moment softened by quiet.

Movement guides the eye and stirs emotion. It invites you to explore a space, noticing how the sunlight dances across a wall or how a sculptural arrangement of tulips stretches and bends unpredictably, the way a curtain billows gently with the faintest breeze or a mirror reflects and reframes your perspective. These touches create energy without chaos, offering moments of discovery within the everyday.

Dynamic design

Introducing movement into a home begins with thoughtful choices. Natural light is a powerful ally, animating interiors as it shifts throughout the day. Amplify this effect with versatile blinds or sheer curtains that let the light in, or by incorporating reflective surfaces that capture and play with illumination. Fresh flowers or foraged branches provide organically sculptural moments - lean into seasonal offerings and choose varieties like poppies, sunflowers or anemones, which add a sense of life and motion with their wayward forms and natural grace.

Furniture placement also plays a role - angle a chair to engage with its surroundings or reposition a floor lamp or the arm of a wall light to create a dialogue between objects. Even the smallest edits, such as turning a jug handle a certain way, adding incense to a holder (even unlit), or leaning a book casually against another on a shelf, can evoke a sense of rhythm, making a space feel more alive and inviting.

Asymmetry: a balancing act

While symmetry can help create moments of elegance – in a bedroom, I personally love the look of matching bedside tables and lamps – it's the asymmetrical details, such as a vase of flowers on one side and artwork on the wall above the other, that introduces energy and intrigue.

These elements, which are not so much about randomness but about harmony, prevent the room from becoming static or predictable. In your living room it could be an oversized armchair opposite a pair of smaller stools, or a large indoor pot plant on one side of the sofa and a low table on the other. It's these intentional irregularities that keep a space feeling fresh and engaging.

The harmony of movement

In music, rhythm is the pulse – a sequence of notes and silences that gives a piece its flow and structure. Without it, melodies lose their way and harmony falters. The same principle can be applied to interior styling. Just as a repeating melody establishes rhythm in a song, repeating elements create a sense of movement and cohesion throughout a home.

As Japanese-American artist and designer Isamu Noguchi said, 'To order space is to give it meaning.' Rhythm in interiors builds on this idea, extending beyond order to guide the eye through a space, introducing moments of interest and fostering harmony. By thoughtfully repeating elements and weaving in varying details, you can establish a rhythm and modulation that ties a room together, much like a well-composed tune. This interplay of repetition and variation breathes life into your home, transforming it into a place that feels both dynamic and balanced.

Ways to establish rhythm in the home

Repetition and variation

Repetition builds continuity, while variation keeps things engaging. You can achieve this by repeating colours, textures or shapes in soft furnishings, furniture or décor. For example, repeating a fabric like soft linen across curtains and bedding can create a cohesive look. Pair this with textural variation – like a wool-upholstered armchair – to add depth. Layer tonal linen cushions, incorporating a hand-painted design or subtle pattern, to introduce visual movement without overwhelming the eye.

Contrast

While variation tends to be subtle, contrasts are more pronounced and can be used sparingly to create impact. Think of pairing dark-toned accents within a neutral palette or juxtaposing organic, rounded forms with straight lines and edges. Offset elements within your material palette – such as smooth marble alongside textured woodgrain. Mixing old and new also creates contrast, like placing a vintage piece with a timeworn patina in a clean, contemporary space.

Radial rhythm

Radial rhythm centres around a focal point, such as a round dining table or a circular rug. Elements arranged around this focal point radiate outward in harmony, creating a striking sense of movement. For example, you could style a round coffee table with layered décor – a central vase surrounded by books or candles in varying sizes – drawing attention to the centrepiece while creating cohesion.

Guiding lines

Lines, whether horizontal, vertical or diagonal, guide the eye and connect elements throughout the space. A horizontal line, such as a low-profile console table or floating shelf, establishes a sense of stability and balance, while vertical elements like tall bookcases or floor-to-ceiling curtains draw the eye upward, enhancing the perception of height. Diagonal lines add energy and movement, and are often found in architectural features like vaulted ceilings with exposed beams. Accentuate these lines with complementary elements, such as a low-hanging pendant light that interacts with the vertical and diagonal lines to bring the space into human scale. The dynamic placement of artwork or furniture can achieve a similar effect, introducing subtle motion and intrigue.

Rhythm in layout

Rhythm isn't just visual; it's about how a space flows and functions. Thoughtful placement of furniture and décor can create zones that feel connected yet distinct, such as defining living and dining areas within an open-plan room. Using rhythm in this way helps ensure that the layout feels purposeful and intuitive, enhancing both the aesthetic and practical experience of the space.

Progression

Gradual changes in colour, size or shape establish a sense of flow. In an open-plan layout, a neutral palette with slight tonal shifts can lead the eye naturally from one space to another. Progression can also be applied to finishing touches. On an open shelf in the kitchen, for example, start with a tall piece, such as an artwork, transition to a medium-sized vase and finish with a smaller stack of cups. Similarly, tableware can be stacked in darker to lighter shades, creating intentional movement across the display.

Natural ease

The principles of the quiet home focus on beauty and calm emerging from restraint. Never overstyled, a quiet home's spaces allow the essence of the house to speak, inviting a slower rhythm and allowing each piece to find its place. They tell the story of a house becoming a home, with items thoughtfully collected over years, yet still leaving room for future layers to unfold. Signs of life - a throw casually draped over a sofa, a stack of books on the floor, the scent of baking, or cups of coffee on the table - bring warmth and soul, reflecting the people who live and gather there. These spaces demonstrate the allure of small, human touches: cushions arranged haphazardly, inviting comfort; an effortlessly dangled lamp cord; the natural crinkle of linen; or the drifting smoke of a blown-out candle.

Embracing the organic beauty of natural textures and handcrafted elements, these interiors honour imperfections and the patina of age, just as nature does. Every piece is meant to be touched, every surface to be used: chairs are for sitting and sofas for stretching out, rugs are to be walked across barefoot and tables are for shared meals and conversation. These rooms offer sanctuary - a gentle balance of simplicity and purpose, where relaxation and lived-in ease blend effortlessly.

A sense of natural ease often evolves over time, shaped by the places we've lived, the lessons we've learned and the memories we've made. It's a mindset that deepens with experience, as we learn to prioritize what truly matters. Rose Tarlow, author of *The Private House*, captures this sentiment beautifully: 'Today, I am far more interested in a home only for myself and those I share my life with. A house is what we design and decorate to suit an image of ourselves, and a home is what we establish by actually living there. To be at home in our house is ultimately the reward of all the effort and thought we put into that most private process of decorating.'

Inviting simplicity

Creating a home with natural ease is about embracing materials, textures and elements that engage the senses and evoke a feeling of simple comfort. It's less about striving for perfection and more about curating spaces that encourage relaxation and connection.

Start by choosing materials that invite touch - sofas and chairs upholstered in soft, tactile fabrics or rugs that feel comforting underfoot. Linen bedding, with its natural drape, adds a sense of effortless elegance. For a touch of quiet luxury, consider swapping a traditional duvet for an oversized linen bedcover that pools elegantly on the floor. Throws made from alpaca or merino wool are perfect for layering on beds, sofas or armchairs, offering warmth and texture, while cushions with feather filling add plump softness.

Be intentional when sourcing pieces for your home. Support conscious brands or local artisans and choose items that celebrate craft and traditional techniques. Handmade ceramics, turned-wood accent pieces and woven fabrics introduce a natural rhythm. Following the enduring wisdom of buying less but buying better helps you to reduce visual noise and make your spaces both personal and inviting.

Take inspiration from nature and your home's surroundings. If you're near the ocean, consider incorporating coastal tones and textures; in leafy areas, draw on earthy hues and organic shapes. Bringing these influences indoors will ground your interiors in a sense of place, creating a seamless connection between the environment and your home.

Sensory elements also play an essential role in fostering natural ease. Scent, for example, can transform a room, adding an invisible layer of refinement. Choose calming fragrances to unwind or uplifting ones to energize. Avoid synthetic scents and look instead to natural candles, essential oils and botanicals - options that create a more authentic and therapeutic atmosphere. When selecting furniture, prioritize comfort. Pieces that offer long, leisurely moments of relaxation will make your home a true retreat - for both you and your guests. A space that goes beyond appearance encourages the simple rituals of daily life, fostering an atmosphere of ease and connection.

The beauty of books

Books hold a unique ability to infuse life into a home, adding layers of meaning, warmth and character. Whether they're displayed prominently or tucked into unexpected corners, they are more than just décor – they reflect who we are and what we love. From gardening and art, to literature and photography, the books we gather weave a narrative of our passions and interests, bringing depth and personality, enriching our spaces and creating a sense of purpose that develops over time.

Shelves lined with well-loved volumes exude a feeling of history and comfort, while stacks of books on coffee tables or even small piles on the floor lend a casual, lived-in aesthetic. A beautifully designed book cover does more than catch the eye – it invites intrigue, sparking curiosity about the stories or ideas within its pages. Regularly changing the books you display brings fresh perspectives and keeps things feeling dynamic. Play around with configurations: for example, create pairings of books at either end of a rectangular table, and nestle them alongside sculptural ceramics, candles or small vases for an effortless, varied and personal touch.

Bookshelves, when styled intentionally, can become focal points in a room. Mix vertical rows with horizontal stacks to add visual interest and balance. For a softer, cohesive look, turn books around to reveal the neutral tones of their pages or remove dust jackets to showcase natural bindings. Add sculptural bookends and layer in decorative items or artworks to add further interest to the arrangement.

Books don't have to be confined to shelves. They can find a home in any corner, from bedside tables to entrance consoles, becoming part of the rhythm of daily life. Whenever I visit a new city, I seek out the best bookshops, but I also love trawling secondhand stores for vintage finds. Over the years, I've uncovered many bargains, particularly in the art genre, where well-worn pages and tatty dust jackets often conceal beautifully preserved hardcovers. These discoveries bring a sense of authenticity to a collection, making it feel meaningful and unique.

Beyond their decorative qualities, books carry an enticing tangible beauty in our increasingly digital lives. Their textures invite touch, their covers spark curiosity and their pages hold the promise of journeys and ideas that inspire. Children's books bring a sense of magic, fostering a love of literature and imagination from an early age. Even as adults, turning pages can be an act of escapism, opening our minds and igniting conversations that linger long after the book is closed.

WHITE
THE TOUCH

Chapter four

Room by room

Through the process of house hushing, we take things away and eliminate the unnecessary. But a quiet home isn't about what's removed, it's about what remains – considered spaces that invite you in with warmth and purpose. Each room offers a chance to infuse personal touches and create a layered, welcoming atmosphere throughout your home, from communal spaces for gathering to quiet corners for solitude. Whether you have compact individual rooms or an airy open-plan layout, various elements of spatial design influence the overall mood of your home. Understanding the function of a space and how it will be used is the first step in reducing visual noise and establishing calm, intentional surroundings. Practical strategies can help you to enhance or adapt to existing constraints, such as a small footprint, limited storage or poor natural light.

Key considerations for every room include existing architectural elements, colour schemes, material finishes, spatial flow, window treatments and lighting. With an understanding of these elements and how to elevate or implement them, along with the thoughtful curation of furniture, rugs and art – and those all-important finishing touches – you'll be well on your way to creating a serene and harmonious home. Always keep sustainability in mind: eco-friendly choices – favouring natural materials, responsible sourcing and longevity over trend-driven pieces – can enhance your interior and support your well-being, reducing waste and contributing to a mindful and visually quiet living environment.

Living room

One of the most frequently used spaces in our home, the living room centres around relaxation. It is a place to embrace the quiet moments of everyday life; it invites us to read or talk, think or watch a movie – activities that instil a sense of peace, grounding us and making us feel safe. A living room can transform from a tranquil retreat for personal downtime, or a solitary space for quiet reflections, into a social hub where we welcome friends and host gatherings. It's a room that works hard – a shared space that must meet the needs of various people as the day unfolds. Whether it's a morning coffee spot, an afternoon play area or an evening sanctuary, it should adapt to the changing pace of life and natural flow of the day.

Given the living room's multifunctional role, a thoughtful and people-centred approach to design and styling is essential to ensure the room can accommodate different moods and different uses, both social and more intimate. By balancing practical needs with the principles of the quiet home – soothing tones, natural elements and soft textures – you can create a space that is warm, relaxed and inviting.

A clean slate

House hushing provides an ideal opportunity to gain a fresh perspective on your living room, allowing you to rethink the space if needed. By clearing out the room, you can familiarize yourself with its footprint without distractions – a clean slate to observe key aspects such as size, shape, ceiling height and the placement of doors and windows. Additional architectural elements like a fireplace, alcove or bay window can also be considered. Understanding these features, along with how you intend to use the space, will help you map out activity zones and circulation paths, guiding your decisions on layout and furniture proportions and placement.

Open-plan living

Many homes have now transitioned to open-plan layouts, favouring fewer walls and open sightlines. This concept merges two or more spaces - most commonly the kitchen, dining and living areas - to better suit our current lifestyles. Open-plan living offers numerous benefits, including enhanced social connections, since it allows family members to engage in conversations and activities while attending to different tasks. When hosting, an open-plan layout enables interaction with guests while preparing meals or drinks. Additionally, open-plan designs improve the flow of natural light and ventilation, contributing to a healthier living environment and overall comfort.

However, adopting an open concept requires careful design considerations to establish sightline boundaries and delineate areas for different uses. While open-plan living has many advantages, homes that maintain defined rooms can provide a sense of place and instil peace and quiet.

If your living room is part of an open floor plan, it's important to consider the entire area, including adjacent spaces, when decorating. While it's not necessary to use identical paint colours and materials, such as wood finishes, throughout, they should complement each other to create a cohesive visual flow. For example, you might choose variations of off-white and neutral tones to maintain a balanced colour palette. Light oak flooring could extend across the whole space, while darker wood accents, such as a coffee table or bookshelves, might tie in with your dining room chairs.

Strategic furniture placement can help delineate the living room within an open-plan space and create zones within large rooms that are cosy and engaging. Start with the sofa, typically the largest piece, and think about how it can be used to mark transitions between spaces. For example, positioning a sofa to face away from the dining room can define the conversation area, creating separation within the open layout. A console placed behind the sofa can further enhance this separation, extend the sofa's presence, and provide space for displaying beautiful objects. Freestanding shelves can also be used as a room divider, while housing books and decorative pieces.

Rather than placing larger furniture like the sofa and armchairs against the walls of the room, consider pulling them in to create a more centralized, floating configuration. This will inject interest and foster an intimate, conversational space, which is especially important if your living room is frequently used for connecting with family and friends. Rugs are a significant layering element for hard flooring, bringing warmth and quiet luxury to the room; they also anchor the furniture, unify the seating arrangement and further define the area. Pay special attention to the size of the rug - it should be large enough for at least the front legs of your sofa and armchairs to rest on it, allowing the entire arrangement to feel cohesive and grounded.

Balancing scale and styling

When choosing new seating, carefully consider the style, size, colour and upholstery, but never compromise on comfort. Sofas are a substantial investment and will receive daily and long-term use, so embrace a slow and mindful approach to finding the right one. Prioritize longevity over trends with timeless, elegant designs and quality craftsmanship. A well-chosen sofa can last for many years, and its life can be extended with new upholstery if needed.

While the size and shape of your living space will largely determine your choice of furniture, play with different scales and heights for visual interest. If the room is small, filling it with lots of small furniture pieces is going to make it feel cluttered. Instead, take a pared-back approach and focus on proportions. For example, pair a generous, low-slung sofa - in a light colour so that it doesn't dominate the space - with a coffee table that is in proportion to the sofa and anchor these pieces on a large rug. Allow for light to flow around the furniture by bringing in some smaller peripheral pieces like side tables or stools that are visually airy.

To conserve floor space with less freestanding furniture, consider built-in solutions that combine shelves to display objects and books, along with closed storage to help manage clutter.

Mirrors can help to amplify a small living room by enhancing and reflecting light. Placed opposite a window, a mirror will create an extension of the view and make the room feel much larger than it is. Choose a minimal style to avoid overpowering the space, but don't be afraid to go big - a tall mirror will create the illusion of height and enhance the overall feel of the room.

When it comes to larger living spaces, resist the temptation to over-furnish. Luxuriate quietly in the volume and embrace negative space.

PICASSO
at 100

Create cosy niches and zones for solitary relaxation or gatherings. Side tables and plinths can be used to display decorative objects like vases, sculptural ceramics and table lamps. These flexible furniture pieces introduce height variation throughout the space, which encourages the eye to travel around the room. They also provide additional surfaces for cups of coffee or wine glasses when entertaining.

To inject character into your living room, lean into contrasts and asymmetrical furniture configurations with a mix of different forms and silhouettes. Consider all styles of seating, including sectional sofas and daybeds, armchairs or a chaise longue. Offset shapes, such as a low-level rectangular coffee table and a taller round side table, and incorporate ottomans and stools for added interest and versatility. They can even function as extra seating for guests.

Accentuate high ceilings with exposed beams and consider adding a low-hanging pendant light to a seating area. This will help create a cosy sense of intimacy by lowering the visual plane. Just be mindful to hang them over a table to avoid any head clashes.

Curated comfort

Remember that the living room is primarily a space to relax, so focus on creating a sensorial, comfortable atmosphere that encourages lingering and conversation - one that feels lived-in and inviting, rather than formal and over-styled. Maintain a minimal, uncluttered space but inject layers of warmth and tactility to engage the senses. Embrace material contrasts and pay attention to soft furnishings - layer your sofa with textured cushions and throws in calm neutral tones and warm earthy hues for added comfort. Display fresh flowers and a scented candle you love on your coffee table, along with stacks of beautiful books. Hang a statement artwork as the focal point of the room, or experiment with different displays of art. This could be a uniform row of small framed photographic art prints in black and white, or an informal gallery wall.

Try not to confine your home to specific periods or styles. Instead, think of it as a thoughtful collection of pieces that hold meaning, rather than a strict exercise in interior design. Always mix some old with the new and make sure the space reflects your personal style, how you like to live and the things that bring you joy.

Layers of light

As natural light moves across a space, it can accentuate architectural elements, creating highlights and shadows to imbue depth and character. In the northern hemisphere, south-facing rooms receive the most consistent natural light throughout the day, making them ideal for living spaces; in the southern hemisphere, the same effect is achieved with north-facing rooms. If you're able to, use these orientations to guide the positioning of your living room and incorporate strategically placed windows and glass doors to invite natural light into the interior.

Make the most of natural light by opening curtains or blinds during the day. At night, create ambience with layered lighting. Instead of overcrowding ceilings with unnecessary downlights, opt for angled ones that create a gentle wall-wash effect. Find a balance of pendant, table, wall and floor lamps, choosing warm-tone bulbs to cast a soft, atmospheric glow in your living room.

Reading nooks

Spaces for solace are inherent to the quiet home concept, but you don't need to set aside an entire room to achieve this. Creating a cosy nook within your living area provides a retreat for quiet reflection, a place to take a break, switch off from technology and get lost in your latest read. Ideally, select a spot that is removed from the main flow of household activity. Consider using a barrier to reduce distractions, such as a room divider, a Japanese-inspired screen, a floor-to-ceiling bookshelf or even an indoor tree.

If possible, choose somewhere with an abundance of natural light, choose comfortable seating such as an enveloping armchair or a daybed layered with cosy cushions and a throw, a side table to keep a drink within easy reach, and either a table or floor lamp for reading at night.

Nooks aren't only for reading; they can be dedicated to any form of relaxation - whether that's listening to music, meditating or practicing yoga. In place of or alongside bookshelves, you might have a music station with a record player and album collection. Or you could reserve space on your rug for morning meditation rituals. Ultimately, these nooks serve as a quiet invitation to slow down, offering a personal retreat that enriches daily life and nurtures your well-being.

Kitchen

The kitchen is the heart of the home – a hardworking space where we prepare meals and gather with family and friends. But with so much activity, this space can easily descend into chaos, especially during high-traffic times like the morning rush or pre-dinner prep. So, how can you maintain a sense of calm even in the busiest moments? The key is striking the right balance between simplifying, maximizing storage, adding warmth and enhancing functionality. Achieving this equilibrium extends beyond aesthetics, resulting in a kitchen that is not only visually pleasing but also a joy to use.

While colour palettes and material finishes are key factors in its design, creating a more restful kitchen begins with thoughtful spatial planning and layout. By improving efficiency, organization and flow, the space will be more streamlined and inviting. Regardless of the size of your kitchen or your budget, it's about making the most of the space – ensuring everything has its place, limiting appliances on the benchtops and keeping cabinets well-organized.

Simple updates for small spaces

Storage is essential for keeping clutter at bay. In a compact kitchen, make the most of vertical space with wall cabinetry. If your existing cabinets are looking tired, consider replacing the doors or giving them a fresh coat of paint. Choose lighter tones to enhance the feeling of space, and either recessed or minimal handles for an elegant finish. Incorporating some open shelving or installing transparent cabinet doors can prevent the kitchen from feeling too closed in, creating an airier feel and providing a place to display meaningful objects, frequently used items and cookbooks. If space allows, consider a compact, freestanding island. A design with raised legs offers a visually lighter expression while adding valuable bench space. If it includes built-in storage, even better.

Starting from scratch

If you're building or undergoing a full renovation, choosing the right location for your kitchen is crucial, since its placement impacts the flow and feel of the entire home. While a kitchen designer can assist with specific layouts, an architect will take a holistic approach to determine the ideal location, considering factors like the best orientation for natural light to create a bright and welcoming space and how it connects to the rest of the house.

The layout you choose should reflect your preferences and how you plan to use the space. Maximize the use of drawers, which offer easier access, better organization and greater capacity than cabinets. You might even eliminate upper cabinetry entirely, opting instead for the simplicity of refined open shelving. If you choose to include a kitchen island, take a minimalist approach, viewing it as a beautiful, uncluttered workbench. Unless you have ample room, carefully consider the necessity of a walk-in pantry; taking space away from the main kitchen isn't always the best option, and generous drawers and cabinets can often be a more efficient use of space.

For larger kitchens with an abundance of room, floor-to-ceiling cabinetry and clean lines can make the kitchen feel seamlessly connected to surrounding areas, especially within a minimalist home. Integrated appliances allows for a cohesive design that extends throughout the space, reducing visual clutter by concealing working areas and mismatched finishes and matching hardware, materials and textures to create a unified and harmonious aesthetic. As a bustling area of the home, the kitchen is inherently filled with audible interactions. Opt for quiet appliances and soft-close cabinets and drawers to minimize noise and maintain a sense of calm.

When planning your kitchen or reworking your home's floor plan, consider adjacent dining spaces and the potential for built-in kitchen nooks, like bespoke seating or bistro tables. If your design includes an island, think about its intended use - will it serve as a breakfast bar, a spot for kids to have their afternoon tea or a gathering area when hosting guests? Depending on your needs, you might choose either a full row of barstools or a pair of stools with additional storage or shelving on one side of the island. Alternatively, you may forgo seating altogether to encourage guests to gather in nearby living or dining areas within an open-plan layout.

EATING OUT LOUD

A peaceful grounding

Flooring sets the foundation for a home's atmosphere, with each room bringing its own set of requirements. In today's open concepts, where the boundaries between cooking, dining and relaxing have blurred, the flooring should seamlessly connect these spaces while meeting the practical demands of everyday life. Prioritize sustainability alongside durability, comfort and insulation, choosing materials that not only endure high foot traffic, spills and varying humidity levels but also contribute to a serene and cohesive environment.

Hardwood floors bring timeless warmth and character, aging beautifully in spaces where elegance and longevity are key. Engineered wood offers a similar aesthetic with added resilience, making it suitable for kitchens with fluctuating moisture levels. Ceramic, porcelain and stone tiles are water resistant and easy to maintain, adding texture and quiet beauty to refined spaces. Cork is an eco-friendly option that provides a soft, warm feel underfoot with natural insulating properties that keep the kitchen cosy in colder months. Reclaimed flooring is another sustainable option, maintaining a sense of history and charm in older homes, and blending heritage with contemporary kitchens.

In open-plan designs, the goal is to create a cohesive look that ties the kitchen and surrounding areas together. Extending the same material throughout these spaces fosters a seamless flow, while combining complementary materials, such as hardwood in living areas and tiles in the kitchen, can add both functionality and visual interest. The best flooring choice supports your lifestyle and enhances the quiet, composed feel of your home, offering a durable foundation that nurtures calm and well-being.

Designing for tranquillity

To cultivate a tranquil and calming atmosphere in the kitchen, embrace soft, muted tones, and keep the material palette concise to maintain cohesion. Prioritize sustainability while adding warmth and texture through timeless, natural materials like wood, marble, stone, bamboo and clay. These elements bring both authenticity and enduring quality to the space.

Keep surfaces uncluttered and focus on a few select areas of the benchtops to create visual interest, such as a floral arrangement or

a sculptural earthenware fruit bowl. Incorporate elements from nature with organic shapes and contrasting textures, crafting vignettes with beautiful everyday items, like a handcrafted wooden chopping board leaned against your splashback, paired with an elegant steel oil pourer and textured ceramic salt dish. Balance the clean lines of kitchen cabinetry and islands with softer forms, such as rounded pottery and barstools, and inject natural textiles into the space. Sheer curtains on surrounding windows or glass doors will bring an elegant touch to the kitchen's framework. Layer flooring with a kitchen runner or mat made from hardwearing natural fibres like jute or sisal.

A visually quiet kitchen speaks a design language that prioritizes peace and comfort, so practice restraint when choosing hardware, tiles and lighting. Opt for discreet handles, and if tiling a splashback, choose neutral tones and avoid overly busy patterns. Lighting should be subtle yet intentional. Consider wall lamps and minimalist solutions above the island like a slimline linear pendant - especially important in open-plan spaces where adjacent dining or living areas may have their own statement pendant lights. Where possible, use LED bulbs and dimmable overhead lighting to adjust the mood for cooking and entertaining.

Creating calm

Not only does an organized kitchen feel more welcoming, but it also transforms daily routines into enjoyable moments. Clutter can quickly overwhelm even the most thoughtfully designed space, so keeping things tidy with well-planned storage will help maintain a sense of order and calm. A well-organized kitchen doesn't just function better - it feels better too. You're more likely to cook, to gather, to linger when everything has its place and purpose. From open shelving to the way you store your dry goods, small changes can have a meaningful impact on how the space flows. Whether your kitchen is compact or you're simply seeking efficiency, the following tips will help you to streamline everything - from decluttering cabinets and drawers to organizing your pantry and fridge.

Storage solutions for an organized kitchen

Declutter

Start by clearing out your pantry, fridge, cabinets and drawers. Remove expired goods, old cookbooks and kitchen gadgets gathering dust. Sort through the odds and ends that are stashed away in high cabinets. Donate those extra mugs, bowls and platters you never use, and give your kitchen room to breathe.

Think vertically

In small kitchens, maximizing wall space is essential. Instead of crowding the area with cabinets, which can feel heavy, consider incorporating open shelving for a lighter, more open look. This also provides an opportunity to display cherished ceramics or art, adding character and visual interest. To maintain cohesion, use the same material finish for your shelves as your cabinetry. To keep benchtops clutter-free, add a hanging rail for utensils or a wall-mounted magnetic knife rack.

Maximize cabinet space

Make deep cabinets more functional by installing pull-out shelves or organizers, so everything is within easy reach. Vertical dividers help keep cutting boards and trays neatly stacked, preventing the frustration of juggling awkward piles.

Organize your fridge

A well-organized fridge ensures mealtimes run smoothly, minimizes food waste and contributes to a more serene kitchen environment. Maximize storage with stackable containers, modular drawers and adjustable shelves. Air-tight BPA-free containers preserve freshness and prevent cross-contamination. Avoid overfilling your fridge, to allow for proper air circulation and consistent temperature control.

Compartmentalize drawers

Use compartments or inserts in drawers to keep cutlery, utensils and kitchen tools in order. Deep drawers are perfect for pots, pans and bulkier items. For safety and a sleek look, consider storing knives in an in-drawer knife block or divider.

Use containers

Organize your pantry by transferring dry goods like flour, cereal and pasta into clear, labelled containers. This not only helps you track your supplies but keeps your shelves looking tidy. Adding racks to the inside of pantry doors is a smart way to store spices and other small items, while freeing up more shelf space.

Store cleaning supplies under the sink
Designate the space under your sink for eco-friendly cleaning supplies and install hooks or racks on the inside of cabinet doors for dish gloves and brushes. If you're renovating, consider integrated bins and recycling solutions to keep everything in one place and out of sight.

Keep benchtops as clear as possible
Reserve benchtop space for meaningful decorative touches that add warmth and character. Simple details like fresh flowers, a natural linen tea towel or a handcrafted ceramic utensil holder can inject personality and charm. Hide charging stations inside drawers to free up even more surface space.

Conceal appliances
Maintain an uncluttered look by reducing the number of appliances on your benchtop. If possible, store items like toasters or blenders when not in use. If you're in the design phase of your kitchen, consider custom-built solutions - such as a concealed coffee bar - and choose fully integrated appliances like fridges and freezers for a sleek, harmonious finish that enhances the sense of calm.

Dining room

Dining rooms have evolved significantly over the past decades. Once a separate and formal space, they have adapted to modern lifestyles with open-plan concepts that blend dining, kitchen and living spaces. Though today's dining table often doubles as a place for working, personal projects or the kids' homework, the core purpose of the dining room remains unchanged - sharing everyday meals with family and hosting larger gatherings. In the quiet home, the dining room plays a pivotal role in promoting a sense of comfort and well-being. It is a space designed to nurture daily rituals, where family and friends can enjoy each others' company and engage in meaningful and enriching conversations over a shared meal or a special celebration; it's where we foster connections and create joyful moments and lasting memories with loved ones.

Spatial harmony

In open-plan living, the challenge lies in ensuring that the dining area is both distinct in its identity and seamlessly integrated with the surrounding spaces. View the entire area holistically, considering spatial dynamics and the room's framework to help you with layout and furniture choices.

When designing, it's essential to understand the room's architectural nuances, since these will heavily influence both the functionality and aesthetic of the space. As you decide on the location of your dining room, consider factors like ceiling height, proximity to the outdoors and any views that could provide a natural backdrop for both casual family meals and more formal gatherings. Pay attention to the flow of foot traffic to ensure easy movement around the space, particularly in open-plan living arrangements. By carefully balancing these elements, you can create a dining space that is both functional and visually harmonious.

Simplicity at Home
WABI-SABI WELCOME

Framing light

If your dining space receives ample natural light, especially from large windows or glass doors, consider that midday meals can take place during the brightest parts of the day. Often, window treatments are an afterthought, but they should be factored into your renovation budget early on since they are essential for controlling light levels and ensuring a cohesive design. They also aid in protecting your furniture from sun damage, such as warping in wooden surfaces or fading in upholstery and rugs. Materials like timber and upholstery are particularly sensitive to temperature fluctuations too, so investing in protective finishes for fabrics and timber surfaces will also help maintain their longevity.

Curtains, blinds and drapes add layers of texture to your dining space, serving multiple purposes. In addition to controlling light levels, they provide privacy during the day. They also contribute to insulation, reduce noise and create ambience in the evenings. Sheer curtains are ideal for dining areas that embody the principles of the quiet home; they offer privacy without blocking out light and lend a relaxed, serene aesthetic - soft and understated, creating warmth without feeling overdone.

For a calming interior, choose neutral tones and natural fibres. Simple linen or soft, gauzy fabrics allow light to filter in beautifully, framing windows without detracting from clean architectural lines. In addition to choosing the right fabric and colour, the style of curtain headings can create distinctive looks. A box pleat, for example, offers a classic, tailored elegance, while a wave pleat introduces a more relaxed feel, especially effective with linen fabrics and sheers. If you're building or renovating, consider floor-to-ceiling curtains hung on concealed recessed tracks. This streamlined, minimalist design offers an effortlessly discreet, floating appearance.

Shaping the space

The dining table is the centrepiece of your space, so evaluate your choice carefully, not based on current trends but on what you love and how it will date. Will the material age gracefully? How will you feel about the design in five, ten or twenty years' time? The material finish of your table is an important consideration, impacting durability and maintenance. Solid wood offers timeless, enduring appeal, developing a beautiful patina over

SERRA

time with only occasional oiling required for maintenance. As well as overall craftsmanship, pay close attention to the design details - including the table legs - which can impact how your chairs fit around the table.

When it comes to shape, rectangular tables work well in long spaces and can accommodate more people when needed. Consider leaving the ends of the table free of chairs for uncluttered, day-to-day use, adding extra seating for larger gatherings. Round tables suit smaller spaces and create a cosy, intimate atmosphere, while oval tables offer the best of both worlds, accommodating more people while maintaining the intimacy of a round table. If space is tight, consider an extendable table so that you can cater for additional guests when required.

Dining chairs offer an opportunity to introduce contrast, texture and character. Comfort is important, especially for long dinners, so prioritize back support and cushioning. The chairs don't need to match, but aim for cohesion in style and materials. For example, you might choose mid-century Danish chairs that feature solid wood frames, some with woven cord seats, and some with leather. Mixing in an armchair or two, or a bench seat, can add variety and interest. Consider upcycling vintage chairs with new upholstery, choosing fabrics that are both durable and beautiful.

Additional furniture pieces that combine functional storage with space to display objects complement the dining area and contribute to the room's calming visual story. A sideboard offers both storage for tableware and linen and an opportunity to create an alluring focal point. Include tactile, sensory pieces such as a grouping of sculptural ceramics, an artwork, floral arrangement, candles or a table lamp. Alternatively, a display cabinet is ideal for showcasing delicate porcelain or collectibles, and a bar cart provides easy access to glasses and drinks while adding a touch of elegance to your dinner parties. Built-in features also work well: consider custom screens or louvres to create separation in open-plan spaces, or a banquette with built-in storage for a stylish and functional seating option.

Set the mood

Establish your colour palette early on with soft, restful tones that carry through from the walls, ceilings and window treatments to everyday staples like table linen and dinnerware. This will provide a subdued canvas against which you can create depth and variation with furniture

and decorative pieces - such as a warm wood dining table, an earthy-coloured rug and verdant blooms - without detracting from the architectural elements of the room.

Inject contrasts but maintain a sense of harmony, with pieces that echo those in adjacent spaces within an open-plan area. For instance, a vintage stainless steel drinks trolley could align with the kitchen benchtops, or a wood sideboard could tie in with the cabinetry.

If the room is self-contained, it should still have a sense of cohesion with the rest of your home, so that the entire house feels interconnected. Take advantage of the wall space in a separate room by hanging a mirror and displaying art. Mirrors work wonders in creating the illusion of space, especially effective if the room is small. Not only does art personalize the interior, creating a focal point and visual interest, but it can also be a wonderful conversation starter at dinner parties. Even if your table is within an open-plan area, located near windows or glass doors, artwork can create impact, while allowing outside greenery to share the limelight.

Placing a rug beneath your dining table will instantly define and enhance the space, acting as an anchor and injecting warmth and texture. Always ensure the rug is large enough to accommodate your chairs, even when they are pulled away from your table. This will prevent them catching on the rug and creating an obstacle for guests.

Set the mood for your space with ambient lighting, considering any surrounding areas that are in view, both indoors and out. For example, how would pendant lighting over the dining table look from every angle, especially if your space is surrounded by glass and outdoor views? Do you need to factor in pendant lights in an adjacent kitchen or living area? This will help maintain a sense of balance and cohesion throughout the space. Lighting fixtures can inject so much character, even when they aren't emitting light. Showcase an elegant pendant by hanging it low but be sure to test it out while sitting at the table. The height should be low enough to create impact, without inhibiting conversation. Create a warm, layered effect by combining different light sources, such as wall sconces, a table lamp on a nearby sideboard and ambient candlelight.

Whether you're hosting a dinner party or enjoying a quiet meal, your table can be a place of beauty, connection and understated charm. With each addition, from the linens and cutlery to the dinnerware and centrepiece, there's an opportunity to craft a setting that feels as calm and inviting as the rest of your home.

Crafting a serene tablescape

Build layers and embrace repetition
Creating an elegant tablescape is a gradual process, one that allows you to slowly build layers and infuse your personal style. View your table as a reflection of your home, a space that evolves over time. There's no need to rush out and buy a full set of matching tableware or glassware. Instead, focus on achieving cohesion through a neutral colour palette and the repetition of elements such as florals and candles. Repetition calms the eye and brings a sense of serenity to your setting.

Choose tableware carefully
If you're considering investing in new dinnerware or linens, opt for quality pieces that can be used for both everyday meals and special occasions. A classic set of dinnerware paired with linens in soft, muted tones offers a versatile base that can be dressed up or down throughout the year. Remember, the food is the hero - your tableware should enhance not overshadow it. Handmade ceramics, organic pieces and vintage finds add character, texture and depth. A beautifully handcrafted serving platter, for example, can elevate the entire setting.

Embrace nature
Let nature guide your tablescape. Draw inspiration from your surroundings and bring a touch of the outdoors in. Seasonal flowers, natural foliage and foraged branches from your garden can add a fresh, organic feel. Whether you choose single stems in bud vases or abundant arrangements as centrepieces, the natural beauty will infuse your table with warmth and texture. The time of year can also influence your theme - consider a more earthy, rustic feel in winter with dark blooms and greenery, or lighter tones in summer for a fresh, airy ambience.

Establish a focal point
A well-chosen centrepiece can anchor your tablescape and draw the eye. Consider a statement candelabra or a floral arrangement as your focal point. Group similar items and play with uneven numbers - three or five - to create a balanced look. Staggering the heights of your pieces and incorporating different textures will add depth and variety. When arranging flowers, keep them low to encourage easy conversation across the table. Candles are essential for setting a warm, inviting mood; their ambient glow will make your guests feel relaxed and at home. Small touches of festivity, such as ornaments or a bit of sparkle at Christmas, can also add charm.

Create elegant place settings
When it comes to place settings, simplicity and elegance go hand in hand. Linens play a big role here – their drape, colour and texture can completely transform the mood of your table. Whether you choose a tablecloth with a standard drape, a full-length drape or a table runner, natural textiles will bring warmth and a relaxed feel. Napkin styling offers endless possibilities: fold them neatly, leave them unfolded for a casual look, place them to the left of the plate or layer them between plates for added texture. For a cohesive look, stick to one or two key colours throughout your table setting, allowing contrasts, such as natural greenery or richly textured ceramics, to add interest.

Add something unexpected
Consider placing a small, unexpected detail at each setting – a fortune cookie, a poem or even a small homemade gift. These thoughtful touches will surprise and delight your guests, making your tablescape not only elegant but also memorable.

Bedroom

Homes that subscribe to a quiet aesthetic effortlessly create spaces for unwinding, reflection and rest, but the bedroom serves as a true retreat. As the most intimate area of the home, it invites a deeply tactile connection, allowing us to relish the comfort of soft sheets and cosy layers while fully switching off and drifting into a peaceful slumber.

Sleep is vital for our well-being. It bolsters our immunity, sharpens focus, aids in memory processing and helps regulate emotions. Without adequate rest, our physical and mental health, as well as our relationships, can suffer. So, how do you create a bedroom that feels like a refuge from the bustle of daily life - a space that fosters restorative sleep and a sense of calm? By applying the techniques outlined in this book, you can visually quieten your bedroom, creating a restful environment that is not only conducive to a good night's sleep, but one that is beautiful and personal.

Fresh perspectives

Start by clearing out your space, viewing it as a blank canvas. This process helps you see the room's potential without the distractions of clutter. Rather than focusing on constraints or aspects you dislike, consider what you can change - especially if renovation isn't an option right now. Something as simple as painting the room or rearranging the furniture can offer a fresh perspective and a sense of renewal.

As you reintroduce items, pay close attention to the flow of movement, ensuring the space is free from obstacles that could disrupt the tranquillity. Observe the architecture of the room. Could you reposition the bed to gain a view of the garden? Do you have a window seat where you could create a reading nook? A thorough declutter makes the room feel more spacious and enhances the sense of calm.

A cohesive palette

The colours you choose for your bedroom significantly influence its mood. Lighter hues layered with warmer, muted tones are ideal for creating a soft, minimalist space. Start with a favourite neutral and weave in subtle variations within that palette. For instance, a mid-beige for the walls and ceiling can be paired with slightly warmer or lighter hues like brown and ecru across bedding, artwork and rugs. Alternatively, you might incorporate earthy greens, warm greys, buttery tones or hints of blue - colours inspired by nature that foster relaxation while adding a personal touch. The goal is to create a pared-back haven where you can relax and unwind. A cohesive colour story, with consistency across design elements, will reinforce a sense of harmony throughout the space.

Painting for impact

Painting is one of the simplest yet most impactful changes you can make. Using one colour across walls and ceilings creates a seamless, calming effect. This technique, often referred to as colour drenching, can make a small room feel larger and more airy, especially when light tones are used. It also eliminates visual breaks in spaces with angled ceilings, preventing a choppy feel. If you want to achieve a cosier, more intimate atmosphere, choose a darker hue to create a cocooning, comforting feel.

For added depth and distinction, use different finishes: matte for walls and ceilings, and gloss or semi-gloss for doors, trims and mouldings. Choose sustainable paints free of harmful chemicals and volatile organic compounds (VOCs) to ensure your sanctuary is both beautiful and healthy. If you are renovating with more extensive updates, consider mineral plaster for the walls - this material absorbs paint pigments and gently reflects softened light, maintaining a minimalist aesthetic that feels warm and welcoming.

Flooring considerations

The flooring you choose will contribute to crafting a tranquil bedroom. Beyond aesthetics, consider durability, sustainability and comfort underfoot. Carpet is a popular choice for bedrooms due to its soft, cushioning fibres, insulating properties and sound-absorbing qualities. However, timber floors offer a timeless, elegant look that adds warmth and character, along with practical benefits like durability and ease of maintenance.

Timber floors are especially beneficial for those with allergies or pets, since they don't trap dust, dirt and allergens the way carpet does. While they may require a higher initial investment, their longevity and ease of cleaning make them a cost-effective choice in the long run. Other alternatives to carpet include engineered wood flooring and eco-friendly options like bamboo and cork, each bringing its unique blend of style and sustainability to the space.

Textural layers

In addition to being long-lasting and versatile, hard flooring can be layered with a rug to help provide thermal and acoustic insulation, creating warmth, interest and depth. Make certain that the size of your rug is suitable for the dimensions of your room and that the placement is conducive to softness underfoot when climbing in and out of bed. Go as big as you can so that both your bed frame and side tables rest entirely on the rug. For a smaller rug, place it under the front two thirds of the bed, to ensure a cosy landing for bare feet. Choose rugs that have been created using fair-trade practices from natural and sustainable fibres such as wool and jute; ones that have some kind of personal meaning or connection will bring you even more joy. So you know how it will feel, it's always better to buy a rug in person, if you can, rather than online.

Bedding plays a pivotal role in transforming your bedroom into a beautiful, restorative space. Support ethical brands and choose sustainable and hypoallergenic bedding materials that are free from harmful chemicals and allergens to promote better sleep and overall health. Natural, fabrics like organic cotton, linen and bamboo offer soft, breathable comfort all year round, and can be layered with cosy wool throws in merino, mohair or alpaca during the cooler months.

Investing in quality bedding allows you to embrace a pared-back approach to styling your bed. The quiet luxury of natural materials, layered effortlessly in muted palettes, becomes the focal point of your bedroom, fostering an inviting and serene atmosphere.

Layering a throw along the end of the bed adds additional texture and a relaxed feel, but exert restraint when it comes to pillows and throw cushions. Too many can overwhelm the space and create practical challenges when finding storage for them overnight. Focus on functionality, comfort and enhancing the room's elegance without detracting from its simplicity.

A headboard creates another opportunity to introduce texture. Choose a tactile fabric that complements your walls and bedding, enhancing the overall colour story by creating a smooth tonal effect or subtle, harmonious contrast.

Clothing and linen storage

While walk-in wardrobes or closets may sound ideal when building or renovating, they require significant space to be truly functional. In smaller rooms, built-in solutions are often more efficient, offering wall-to-wall storage for clothes, shoes and linen. The design should reflect your personal needs – incorporating hanging racks for longer dresses and coats, along with open shelves for easy access to folded garments, and closed storage for smaller items.

Doors contribute to both the functionality and overall aesthetic of the space. Choose lightweight options that are easy to open and close while offering ventilation. Doors painted in the same colour as the walls create a seamless effect, or you can introduce contrast with warm wood or textured fabric panels. For the finer details, minimalist finger-pulls add a sleek finish, while handles such as antique bronze knobs or contemporary wood options enhance the room's style and character.

Light layering and control

While natural light during the day is life-giving, having the ability to control it for privacy and sleep is crucial. The right window treatments not only allow you to regulate light according to your needs, but they also enhance the tactile, soothing atmosphere of the space. When selecting curtains or blinds, focus on finding a solution that blends effortlessly with the room's interior since this will provide a soft and calming effect. Bold or busy patterns can quickly add visual noise, detracting from the serene environment you want to create. Instead, explore materials and textures in neutral colours, focusing on a balance of beauty and functionality.

Consider the architecture of your home when choosing window treatments. Blinds or shutters can effectively block light and provide privacy, while curtains add warmth and softness. Combining different treatments, like layering sheer curtains with heavier drapes or pairing shutters with light curtains, allows for a more versatile and personalized approach to light control.

If you require blackout curtains for optimal sleep quality, consider pairing them with sheers. Falling gracefully, sheers soften the light without completely blocking it, creating an ethereal quality during the day. Additionally, playing with scale can enhance the feeling of space in your bedroom. For instance, pairing longer curtains with smaller windows can make the windows appear larger and the room more expansive.

Bedroom lighting should be layered and warm - a gentle glow that supports relaxation and rest. Bedside table lamps or wall sconces provide adequate lighting for reading; if possible, install dimmer switches beside the bed for ease of use. Lighting scented candles adds a calming, sensory element to the room, helping you to relax and prepare for sleep. Switching off from technology and screens is equally important in creating a peaceful atmosphere. Keep laptops and phones elsewhere overnight and instead read a book or listen to relaxing music to help you wind down.

A personal sanctuary

To make the bedroom truly your own, pay attention to details and finishing touches. Infuse character into the space with carefully curated pieces that hold meaning for you. Whether it's sculptural bedside tables, a beautiful vintage dresser passed down from a family member, a custom headboard

upholstered in gorgeous, textured fabric, or elegant bedside lamps, these elements contribute to a room that feels uniquely yours.

Older furniture pieces can be revived with new hardware or upholstery, such as replacing handles on beside tables or recovering an occasional chair for the corner of the room. Whether you use the chair for reading, putting on shoes or simply as an added surface for books and draping clothes, it provides another opportunity to inject character and make your mark. A bench seat at the end of the bed is also a nice touch offering both practicality and visual interest.

Art is a powerful way to evoke emotion and add a unique element to your bedroom. Choose pieces that resonate with you personally, creating a connection that makes the space feel intimate and special. This might be a serene landscape, an abstract work in soothing tones that brings calm and relaxation, or a photograph or painting of a place you love - a reminder of a cherished memory. Whether you select a large statement piece as a focal point above the bed or a smaller work that quietly enriches the space, art can instil your bedroom with a sense of quiet luxury and individuality.

Bathroom

Bathrooms have unique requirements, and functionality often takes precedence over aesthetics, but they also provide an opportunity to create a beautiful, engaging sanctuary that elevates daily living. Our bathrooms are where we get ready for the day ahead and unwind in the evening, where we cultivate personal rituals for self-care and relaxation. A functional layout and considered design elements will help streamline these daily routines, enhancing the efficiency at which we can get ready to go about our day, while at the same time creating a calming place that soothes and rejuvenates.

Start by decluttering and clearing out all unnecessary excess, including expired or unused bathroom products. Adequate storage helps keep benchtops clear, allowing a few essentials like hand soap, with other items neatly tucked away. Use compartmentalized drawers and baskets inside cabinets to help keep everything organized. In smaller bathrooms, think vertically: install robe hooks, and consider floating furniture to create a more open feel. Wall-hung vanities with exposed plumbing work particularly well in tight areas, especially powder rooms. In primary bathrooms, maximize space by creating distinct zones, such as a combined bath and shower area. Mirrors and reflective surfaces like marble, glass and metal facilitate the flow of light, further enhancing the feeling of spaciousness.

A spa-like retreat

A spa visit can provide a much-needed pampering session to de-stress when life gets busy, following a particularly draining week or as a general pick-me-up. From rejuvenating facials and massages, through to immune-boosting saunas and ice baths, day spas offer a myriad of treatments that benefit both the mind and body. But much of the allure of a spa comes from the aesthetics of the space and the culmination of tactile, sensory elements - many of which can be replicated at home.

Creating a spa-like bathroom begins with a restful colour palette and a focus on materiality. For a cohesive look, select colours that align with the rest of your home's interior - muted, calming tones inspired by nature, especially those reminiscent of earth and sand, are in fitting with the refined luxury of a spa environment. Natural materials such as stone lend an organic, grounded feel; while stone is often thought of in neutral shades, stunning slabs in soft hues like blush or rose can add a subtle touch of colour. Marble, with its tactile appeal and variety of dense veining, pairs beautifully with rich woodgrains to create immersive, quietly luxurious spaces. When selecting finishes, take the time to research both natural and engineered options to find durable, low-maintenance materials that suit your needs.

Offset clean lines with rounded forms such as sculptural tapware/faucets and light fixtures, and look for special details that add character, like handmade tiles or vintage mirrors. To inject warmth and comfort during the colder months, consider heated towel rails and underfloor heating - they'll make stepping out of the shower on a chilly winter morning much more enjoyable. Gather samples and curate a mood board to help consolidate your choices, ensuring there is harmony and cohesion throughout.

For textural wall finishes, tadelakt - a traditional Moroccan lime plaster - offers a warm, seamless finish that is soft and undulating to the eye with a gentle sheen. Naturally resistant to mould and mildew, its lime-based composition makes it ideal for minimalist wet-area applications. While it requires skilled application, when done correctly and with regular upkeep to maintain its water-resistant properties, it can last for decades. For a similar aesthetic with more durability and less maintenance, microcement provides a beautiful alternative and can also be used for flooring.

If you simply want to bring a spa-like feel to your existing bathroom, or you're working with limited space or budget constraints, there are many ways to enhance tranquillity. A fresh coat of paint can make a big difference, with specialty paints like lime wash offering warm, textural finishes that mimic the look of tadelakt and microcement. Designed for wet areas and able to withstand high humidity while being naturally anti-bacterial and mould-resistant, lime-wash paint is ideal for refreshing walls while contributing to a healthier environment. Applied over conventional paint, it adds visual depth and warmth, softening hard finishes and bringing texture to minimalist spaces.

For a simpler solution to updating tiles without a full renovation, there are specialty paints that can be applied directly over them, allowing you to tone down colours with ease. Upgrading bathroom handles or tapware/ faucets can also breathe new life into the room - look for elegant shapes and tactile finishes like brushed stainless steel or natural brass. Replacing your shower head with a rainfall design, even in smaller showers, can offer a more relaxing, spa-like experience.

To further elevate your daily rituals, choose natural products free from artificial fragrances, and invest in quality towels made from certified organic cotton - soft, absorbent and ethically sourced. Place a small wooden stool or side table beside the bath to keep items like a book, essential oils or a candle within reach. An over-the-tub tray can also add a luxurious touch to your soak.

Brighten the room with fresh greenery or seasonal flowers. By focusing on sensory elements and embracing quiet luxury, you'll create an inviting space for daily rituals - a place you'll enjoy spending time in.

Light-filled sanctuaries

As modern living has evolved, multiple bathrooms - en suite, powder rooms and even dedicated children's spaces - have become the norm in contemporary homes. While adding extra bathrooms can be a priority as families grow or the need for more space arises, integrating them into older homes poses unique challenges, especially when it comes to accessing natural light. Even in new builds, bathrooms often take a back seat to bedrooms in terms of placement along highly prized exterior walls, reducing their access to natural light and fresh air. This can result in small, dark spaces that lack the many benefits that natural light provides for our well-being.

When designing a new floor plan, prioritize natural light from the outset. Make your bathroom windows as large as possible and use minimal window treatments - such as sheers or blinds - that allow light to permeate while still providing privacy. Make sure window coverings are easy to adjust, giving you control over the amount of light that enters the space. Skylights can be a beautiful addition, drawing direct light from above and enhancing the connection to nature. They also come in various forms - vented, tinted or combined with automatic shutter systems - offering flexibility in both light and ventilation.

While privacy often dictates the layout of bathrooms, avoid solid walls that can block the flow of light, and make even spacious bathrooms feel enclosed. Consider open shower designs with frameless glass doors or screenless wet areas to create an airy feel. High-level clerestory windows or skylights positioned over the shower can bring in additional light without compromising privacy. Placing your bath near the window with views of nature will enhance the spa-like feel of the space.

Natural light can reduce the need for artificial lighting during the day, but well-considered lighting is crucial for morning and evening routines. Aim for a layered approach that balances functionality with ambience – gentle lighting to ease into the day and wind down at night. Be mindful of placement, especially around the vanity, where lights should softly illuminate your face from all angles, avoiding the harshness of overhead fixtures. Remember, lighting solutions are more than functional; they are integral to the room's design aesthetic, even when switched off. Select pieces that enhance the serene, tranquil atmosphere of your space, such as sculptural, minimalist sconces and dimmable pendants. Choose materials like brushed metal or natural stone to bring tactile, organic touches to the space.

Home office

The way we work has changed considerably over the years, with many of us now working from home at least part of the week. Advances in technology have allowed us to become more nomadic, often requiring little more than a laptop and somewhere to perch. While the flexibility of this may sound enticing, the boundaries created by a dedicated workspace are far more beneficial to our sense of calm and well-being. Without them, the distractions of home can disrupt our focus and productivity, blurring the lines between work and the valuable time needed to switch off, relax and connect with family. Whether you're working from home full-time or a few days a week, or you simply need to manage household affairs, a defined space to do it in is essential for maintaining both workflow and a sense of order. And while it can take many forms - a spare bedroom, a corner of the kitchen, an attic conversion or even a standalone studio - there are plenty of ways to create a workspace that feels personal, well-organized and inspiring.

An intentional workspace

While many contemporary homes feature a built-in office or study, those living in older homes often face a decision: transform an unused area into a functional place to work or extend the home to create a new office. Begin by determining your workspace needs. How much room and privacy do you require? Will you need a table and chairs for meetings, or do you anticipate frequent video calls? Is ample storage a necessity? If you don't have a spare room to convert into a private office, consider an underused corner of a bedroom. If the space will only be used as an office a couple of days a week, could it double as a guest bedroom? You might incorporate a fold-down bed or create a window nook with a desk. Alternatively, look at converting an area within your living room, using a curtain or screen as a partition. Remember, our homes should be adaptable, evolving with us as our situations change - whether due to

a growing family or a career shift that necessitates working from home. The office space is another piece of the puzzle, a step in the journey where new memories can be created, contributing to the story of our lives.

Design for well-being

When planning your home office, let natural light guide your decision on where to convert or borrow space. Exposure to natural light is vital for maintaining our circadian rhythms – the 24-hour cycle that regulates our internal body clock and impacts our physical and mental well-being. If possible, position your desk near a window to harness natural light, which will boost both mood and productivity. During early mornings, evenings and the darker winter months, balance ambient lighting to brighten the space with task lighting for focused activities. A combination of a pendant or floor lamp paired with a desk lamp creates a warm, layered feel that is well suited to a calming home office.

Designing a workspace that feels good starts with choices that nurture both you and your surroundings. Select non-toxic paints and embrace natural materials like wood, stone, linen, wool and sisal – these not only add warmth but also support a healthier environment. Keep fresh air flowing with regular ventilation and consider air purifiers or humidifiers to further enhance the space. Introducing plants brings a touch of nature indoors, and lifts your mood.

Quality acoustics will help minimize disruptions and nurture your overall state of mind. Incorporate noise-reducing elements like heavy curtains to block out external noise and soft textile elements like rugs and cushions, which help dampen sound. Features such as wall-to-wall bookshelves and strategically placed plants not only elevate your room's aesthetics but also absorb and diffuse sound, enhancing the acoustics of your workspace.

The furniture pieces you choose for your home office should be well considered in terms of functionality. Contemporary desks cater to modern living with innovative options such as charging accessories and height-adjustable mechanisms to allow for standing. Meanwhile, ergonomic chairs provide optimal comfort and encourage movement. However, functional pieces needn't compromise on style – the iconic Eames Management Chair is a perfect example. Celebrated for its comfort, elegance and versatility, it continues to be a favourite worldwide, in large

design-conscious offices and compact home setups alike. Desks anchor the space and offer opportunities to showcase beautiful design, materials and craftsmanship. Consider options like a vintage desk with built-in drawers or open shelves, or a repurposed dining table. Alternatively, explore custom built solutions to accommodate nooks, alcoves or awkwardly shaped rooms. A wall-mounted floating desk is sleek and minimal without occupying floor space, making it perfect for small offices.

If you have a larger home office that can accommodate more than just a desk for focused work, create zones for different tasks, such as a comfortable armchair for reading and a table for meetings and jobs that require spreading out. A corner for peaceful moments can provide necessary respite throughout the day. Cultivate a balance between visually uplifting elements to foster workflow and more subdued surroundings for quiet interludes. Taking regular breaks is essential for maintaining a sense of well-being. Stepping outside for fresh air can be a great way to reset, and if you can, incorporate light exercise and stretching breaks into your day to help maintain your energy levels and keep your mind engaged.

Decluttering for mental clarity

Whether you're setting up a home office or enhancing an existing space, maintaining an organized, clutter-free environment is key to promoting mental clarity and emotional well-being. Choose storage solutions that are both practical and visually appealing – think versatile bookshelves, wall-mounted open shelves above your desk, or a sideboard with concealed cupboard space. Prioritize simplicity in design and materials that bring warmth and understated elegance to your workspace. Cultivate systems that offer easy access to frequently used items, hidden storage for equipment like printers, and space to display objects that reflect your personal style. Surrounding yourself with items that inspire and uplift will help you foster a space that nourishes your emotional state.

Pay attention to the details that enhance efficiency and maintain order. Use sleek, minimal desk accessories such as trays and pen holders to keep your desk clear and tidy. Streamline technology by managing cables well and opting for wireless devices, when possible, to reduce the clutter of cords. Aim for a paperless filing system or use file organizers to keep important documents neatly stored. Establish a routine for staying

VERTONE
JUST A NOTH
AKIO MAKIGAWA

organized - take a few minutes at the end of each workday to tidy your desk, sort through papers and return items to their designated spots. This habit will help you start each day with a clear and focused mind.

Personal touches

One of the unique perks of working remotely is the freedom to craft an office that reflects your personal story - a space that feels connected to your home while maintaining a sense of separation and its own distinct purpose. The goal is to design a workspace that not only complements the overall style of your surroundings but also welcomes you each day with a sense of calm and focus. It's about creating an environment that feels personal and inspiring, a place where you can truly do your best work.

Surround yourself with objects that hold meaning and bring comfort - pieces that speak to you and contribute to the narrative of your home. A vintage lamp, a cosy rug underfoot, a sculptural ceramic vessel or an artwork that resonates can all enhance the mood of the space. What you choose to include should feel intentional, reflecting both your personal style and what inspires you.

By weaving together functional design, natural elements and meaningful details, you can shape a space that nurtures both your productivity and your well-being.

Further reading

Gaston Bachelard
The Poetics of Space
Penguin Random House | Penguin Classics, 2014

Hans Blomquist
The Natural Home
Ryland, Peters & Small, 2012

Ilse Crawford
A Frame for Life: The Designs of Studioilse
Rizzoli, 2014

Matt Gibberd
A Modern Way to Live: 5 Design Principles from The Modern House
Penguin Random House | Penguin Life, 2021

Shira Gill
Minimalista
Mitchell Beazley | Octopus Publishing Group, 2021

Ali Heath and Lynda Gardener
Curate
Mitchell Beazley | Octopus Publishing Group, 2021

Kinfolk & Norm Architects
The Touch: Spaces Designed for the Senses
Gestalten, 2025

Colin King, with Sam Cochran
Arranging Things
Rizzoli, 2023

Leonard Koren
Wabi-Sabi: For Artists, Designers, Poets & Philosophers
Imperfect Publishing, 2008

Karen McCartney, Sharyn Cairns and Glen Proebstel
Perfect Imperfect: The Beauty of Accident, Age & Patina
Allen & Unwin | Murdoch Books, 2016

Norm Architects
Soft Minimal: A Sensory Approach to Architecture & Design
Gestalten, 2022

Anna Potter
Flower Philosophy: Seasonal Projects to Inspire and Restore
Quarto Group | White Lion Publishing, 2023

Juhani Pallasmaa
The Eyes of the Skin: Architecture and the Senses
John Wiley and Sons, 2024

Rick Rubin
The Creative Act: A Way of Being
Canongate Books, 2023

Chrissie Rucker and The White Company
For the Love of White
Mitchell Beazley | Octopus Publishing Group, 2019

Deyan Sudjic
John Pawson: Making Life Simpler
Phaidon Press, 2023

Junichiro Tanizaki
In Praise of Shadows
Penguin Random House | Vintage Classics, 2001

Rose Tarlow
The Private House
Rizzoli, 2024

Rose Uniacke
Rose Uniacke at Work
Rizzoli, 2023

Index

Picture credits

Every effort has been made to trace all copyright owners but if any have been inadvertently overlooked, the publishers would be pleased to make the necessary arrangements at the first opportunity.

Front cover Photography: Helen Cathcart; design: MURUDÉ studio murude.com **Back cover** Photography: Nicole Franzen; interior design: Corinne Mathern Studio.

With special thanks to Ask og Eng for their images on pages 12, 37, 41, 70 and 204.

2 Photography: Michelle Halford; **7** Photography: Dave Wheeler; interior design: Phoebe Nicol; **8** The home of Nicolas and Charlotte Horsch of Horsch & Huebescher; photography Joachim Behr; **11** Rug: Nordic Knots; photography: Felix Odell; **15** Photography: Timothy Kaye; Architecture and interior design: Odyssey Architecture; styling: @nicola__rogers; **19** Photography: Kristofer Johnsson; styling: Amanda Rodriguez; **20-21** Photography: Harry Crowder; interior design: Robert London Design; **23** Photography: Jonas Bjerre-Poulsen; architecture and design: Norm Architects; **25** Photography: Emma Jönsson Dysell (Harvest Agency); interior design and styling: Malin Wahlström Walter; **26** Photography Irina Boersma; interior design Kate Imogen Wood; **27** Photography: Marianne Jacobsen; **28** Photography: Nina Helland Sortland @nina_notetoself; **29** Photography: Sandie Lykke Nolsøe; architecture and design: Norm Architects; **30** Photography Nicole Franzen; interior design: Corinne Mathern Studio; **33** Design: Avenue Design Studio www.avenue-designstudio.com; **35** Photography: Patric Johansson; styling Myrica Bergqvist; **36** Photography: Kristofer Johnsson; styling: Shalony van Stralendorff; **38** Photography: Marieke Verdenius; interior design: Hum Studio & Gallery; **42** Photography: Andrea Papini for Nordiska Kök; styling: Anna Furbacken; **44** Photography: Michelle Halford; **47** Photography: Helen Cathcart; design: MURUDÉ studio murude.com; **48** Photography: Nicole Franzen; interior design: Corinne Mathern Studio; **51** living4media/View Pictures; **52** Photography: Jonas Berg; styling: Emma Fisher and Annica Clarmell; **54** The Arnold Madsen Clam Chair by Dagmar; Photography: Irina Boersma César Machado; styling: Pernille Vest; **55** Photography: Helen Leech; interior design: All & Nxthing; **56-57** The Strata 1600 pendant by J. Adams & Co; **58** Photography: Michelle Halford; **61** Photography: Kristofer Johnsson; interior architecture: wtp studios; **62** Photography: Erik Lefvander; styling: Pella Hedeby; **63** Photography: Andrea Papini for Nordiska Kök; styling: Marie Graunbøl; **64** Photography: Studio Periphery; interior design: Pupil Office; **66-67** Jake Curtis/Future Publishing Ltd; **69** Photography: Ondrej Holub @okemhome; **71** Sector desk: Ferm Living; **73** Photography: Michelle Halford; **75** Photography: Kristofer Johnson; interior design: AO/JN Interiors Project "G138"; **76** Photography: Thomas De Bruyne; interior architecture: Jim Dierckxe; **77** Architecture and photography: Christian Brailey Architects; **79** Abstract rug: Ferm Living; **80** Photography: Mikael Lundblad; **81** Photography: Nicola Helgesen and Andreas Beckmann for oldtownhaus; **83** Photography: Helen Leech; interior design: All & Nxthing; **84** Pure linen bedding: By Mölle www.bymolle.com; **86** Nina Helland Sortland @nina_notetoself; **87** Photography: Jake Curtis; Styling: Abi Boura; creative direction: Rozzi Stanford; **88** Photography: Lauren Miller; interior design: Kessler Levitan Design; **91** Photography: Erik Lefvander; interior design and styling: Pella Hedeby; **93** Nordiska Kök at Lotta Klemming's Ostrongården; **94** Photography: Thomas De Bruyne; interior architecture: Jim Dierckx; **97** Photography: Michelle Halford; **98** Arum lamp: Ferm Living; **101** Photography: Mikael Lundblad; styling: Emma Wallmén; **102** Photography: Simon Brown; architecture and design: De Rosee Sa; **103** Photography: Rebecca Goddard; **105** Reed vitrine: Ferm Living; **107** Tapestry blanket: Ferm Living; **109** Design: Avenue Design Studio www.avenue-designstudio.com; **111** Simone Polk Artist @simonepolk; **112** Photography: Sandie Lykke Nolsøe; architecture and design: Norm Architects; **113** Chair and side table: Audo Copenhagen www.audocph.com; **115** Photography: Owen Gale, House & Garden, ©Condé Nast; the home of Laura Logan @house_of_logan; **116** The Arnold Madsen Clam Chair by Dagmar; Photography: Christian Moller Andersen; styling: Marie Graunbol; **118** Photography: Lynden Foss; styling: Nathalie Walton; **119** Photography: Dean Hearne, Design: Works Architecture; **120** Photography: Lauren Miller; design: TwoFold Interiors; **122** Design: Kate Imogen Wood, Ferm Living; **123** Simone Polk Artist @ simonepolk; **125** Photography: Ryan McDonald; interior design: AZL Interiors; **126** Simone Polk Artist @simonepolk; **127** Photography: Helen Leech; interior design: All & Nxthing; **128-129** Photography: Dario Borruto; project design: Opus Atelier; **131** Design: Ferm Living; **133** Photography: Salva López; design: Andrew Trotter and Marcelo Martínez; **134** Photography: Nicole Franzen; interior design: Jute Interior Design; **137** Photography: Abi Dare; **138** Photography: Michelle Halford; **141** Photography: Kristofer Johnsson; styling: Sophie Brunner; **142** Photography: Nina Holzst; **145** Photography: Melanie Jenkins; styling: Michelle Halford for Baya www.bayaliving.com; **146-147** Design: Ferm Living; **148** Photography: Thomas De Bruyne; interior design: Nathalie Deboel; **151** Photography: Nicole Franzen; interior design: Bespoke Only; **153** Photography: Andrea Papini for Nordiska Kök; styling: Marie Graunbøl; **154** Photography: Andrea Papini for Nordiska Kök; styling: Anna Furbacken; **156-157** Photography: Nic Gossage; architecture and interior design: Michiru Higginbotham; **159** Photography: Felix Speller; Kitchen Furniture Design: Edward Collinson; interior design: BWT Interiors; styling: Hannah Franklin; **160** Photography: Timothy Kaye; interior design: CJH Studio; **163** Photography: Marieke Verdenius; **165** Photography: Mart Goossens for Flare Department; interior design: Interior Studio van Maanen, Like Home & ROCK Development; styling: Like Home; **166** Photography: William Jess Laird; interior design: Bespoke Only; **168** Photography: Kristofer Johnsson; styling: Sophie Brunner; **170** Photography: Studio Periphery; interior design: Pupil Office; **173** Photography: Marieke Verdenius; **175** Photography: Helen Leech; interior design: All & Nxthing; **176** Photography: Nicola Helgesen and Andreas Beckmann for oldtownhaus; **177** Photography: Jake Curtis; fabrics and accessories: de Le Cuona; **179** Photography: Helena Nord; styling: Pella Hedeby for Watt&Veke; **180** Interior design: OOAA www.ooaa.es @ooaa_arquitectura; **181** Photography and styling: Eszter Karpati; **183** Photography: Kristofer Johnsson; styling: Sophie Brunner; **184** Design: Ferm Living; **185** Offset bedspread: Ferm Living; **186-187** Interior: Audo Residence, Copenhagen www.audocph.com; **189** Photography: Helen Cathcart; design: HUTCH; **190** Photography: Sean Fenessy; interior design: Emily Gillis; **193** Photography: Flare Department; interior design: Carl Devin Wesselius, Studio Asker; **194** Photography: Salva López; architectural and Interior Design: Studio Andrew Trotter www.andrew-trotter.com; **195** Design: Vermland www.vermland.dk; **197** Woodstock Flip Top Table and Arena 4 Star Chair with Castors, both by Icons of Denmark; **199** Photography: Jonas Bjerre-Poulsen; architecture and design: Norm Architects; **200** Photography: Jonas Bjerre-Poulsen; architecture and design: Norm Architects; **202** Photography: Michelle Halford; **203** Photography: Michelle Halford.

Michelle Halford is an interior stylist and designer who has created calm and quiet spaces for numerous high profile clients including Nespresso, Dulux and BoConcept. Her work has appeared in many publications in her native New Zealand and around the world. You can follow her on Instagram @thedesignchaser or online at thedesignchaser.com